ENCOUNTER

Published by The Disciples Center for Education
125 Spring Hill Drive
Boerne, TX 78006
Info@disciplescenterforeducation.org
www.disciplescenterforeducation.org

Design by Josie Ziegler
E111523

Contents

Introduction

"You have said, 'Seek my face.'
My heart says to you,
'Your face, Lord, do I seek.'
Hide not your face from me."
Psalm 27:8-9

When we think about encounters with God, they might seem sudden, accidental, or at least out of our control. We're just living life, and then suddenly, we're struck by a moment of awe or changed by a Spirit-initiated epiphany. While encounters with God can certainly occur when we least expect them, we will more likely experience God in new and exciting ways if we deliberately seek out such an encounter. Like David, we can set our hearts on seeing His face.

The scriptures are filled with examples of men and women encountering God, and no two encounters are alike. Jacob wrestled with God. Hannah prayed silently and wept bitterly. Paul was blinded and rebuked on the road to Damascus. These, and other encounters, may seem like the sudden type of God meeting. But they share similar characteristics. There's a before, a during, and an after.

Let's use Abraham as an example. In Genesis 22, Abraham is minding his own business with Isaac, the son of the promise, when God sets him up for an encounter by telling him to go up Mount Moriah to sacrifice his son. As Abraham faithfully lifts the knife, he encounters an angel of the Lord who tells him to stop and use a ram caught in a thicket. After the encounter, Abraham and Isaac (no doubt relieved!) walk back down the mountain with a new blessing and a new outlook.

As we seek to encounter God, we'll follow a similar trajectory: Ascent, Encounter, Descent. These three aspects of encounter are captured in the simple graphic below that also represents the three sections of this devotional booklet. The first section, Ascent, will prepare your heart for the encounter experience. The Encounter section will guide you on your personal retreat with God. The last section, Descent, will transition you off the mountain and back into life with lasting change. Each section is previewed below.

Ascent

Begin 15 days before your Encounter retreat

We all want the mountain top experiences, but we often forget that climbing a mountain is hard. The people of Israel were expected to attend three festival weeks a year in Jerusalem. Many Jews who lived in other parts of Israel would faithfully pack up belongings, children, and sacrifices in order to make the pilgrimage to Jerusalem and its temple on Mount Zion as often as possible. (And sometimes they would head for home and forget one of their children – Luke 2:41-52.)

The elevation of Mount Zion meant that any such trip involved a good deal of climbing. Maybe you've noticed that some of the Psalms (120-134) have the subtitle A Song of Ascents. Have you ever wondered what that meant? Well, the *Songs of Ascents* were the Psalms that may have been sung on the way up (the ascent) to Jerusalem for festival by Jews who returned from exile in Babylon. They may have even used these songs to re-enact their return from exile. We'll imaginatively read these fifteen Psalms as if they are a "pilgrim's playlist" for anyone seeking to go up and be with God.

So, as we set out for our encounter with God we will be ascending with the songs of this pilgrim's playlist. As you'll see, each Psalm deals with a unique aspect of our hearts as we get closer and closer to an encounter with God on the top of the mountain. We'll follow the **storyline** of the Psalm: what does this Song of Ascent tell us about the God that we are on our way to meet? And we will follow the **lifeline**: how can our bodies, minds, hearts, and souls begin to practice the presence of God as we draw nearer to the summit?

*It may take you more than fifteen days to complete the Ascent devotionals. Go at your own pace. The important thing is connecting with God.

Encounter
Plan Now

After completing fifteen devotionals, readying our hearts, and marching up toward God, we'll have a special meeting with God called The Encounter. There are some things you'll need to do in advance to get the most out of this experience. (One of those things is to take the pressure off getting the most out of this experience. God will lead you.)

- Set a date for your encounter and begin the Ascent daily devotionals fifteen days before your set date. (It's okay if you go on retreat before you finish the Ascent portion.)
- There are not many rules for what this looks like except making intentional time, alone, with you and God. You could:
  - Rent an AirB&B or cabin
  - Go camping, hiking, or to the beach
  - Send your kids to grandma's so you can encounter God at home
  - Fly to Jerusalem and visit the Holy Land (You probably can't do this, but it would be epic.)
- Decide if you will spend ½ a day, a whole day, or (ideally) 2 days away with God – The Encounter is flexible.
  - The more time you can spend, the better. But the most important thing is just to spend some time, even if it's not as much as you would want.
  - You'll build your own Encounter plan that will fit whatever length you can commit to.
- This would be a good time to put this booklet down, take out your calendar, and plan when you'll do your Encounter.

  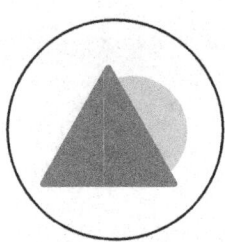

Descent

The 15 days after your Encounter retreat

No one stays on the mountaintop. The highest heights can be awe-inspiring and spectacular, but they are not permanent. Mountain climbers know that they can only stay on the peak for so long before making their descent. Christians know this too. If you've ever been to a church conference or camp, or gone on a mission trip, then you know that the euphoria of fellowship, worship, or serving those in need is fantastic but fleeting. Even those worshipers who ascended Mount Zion, singing Psalms, had to go back to their communities after the festival ended. I imagine they had so much to reflect on and talk to one another about as they journeyed home after a special time with God. Those moments on the way down from the mountain had the potential to be just as formative as the encounter itself. In that sense, the descent is very important. The lessons from your encounter need time to sink in. The ideas that God places on your heart need to be massaged into your soul.

On the day after your encounter, you'll begin a new set of fifteen daily devotionals designed to bring you down from your time with God and back into the world with a lasting impression of your encounter. Scripture is full of mountaintop experiences with God. We've probably heard many sermons with points drawn from those encounters. These devotionals take a different approach. We'll look at the post-encounter narratives of fifteen individuals in the Bible. We may be familiar with what happens on the highest heights, but do we know how God changes his people in the aftermath of encountering him? These storylines will help you process your time with God. The lifelines will encourage you to open your mind, heart, body, and soul to new experiences and new postures with God.

Ascent

15 Days before your Encounter

Woe to me, that I sojourn in Meshech, that I dwell among the tents of Kedar!
Psalm 120:5

Storyline: Read Psalm 120

The pilgrim's playlist for the journey up to Mount Zion begins with a song of distress. This is often the starting point for those seeking an encounter with God. Sure, we feel called by God to come up and meet him, but we may feel equally compelled to do whatever it takes just to get out of wherever we currently are. Every journey has a starting point. Try not to judge your starting point. It is important to recognize where you are and accept it.

As the Psalmist laments his current situation, he mentions two locations that are almost certainly symbolic. Meshech means to be drawn out. Kedar means darkness. Because of the current struggle that the Psalmist is experiencing, he feels like he's been hiding in the darkness. Now, as he cries out to God at the beginning of this journey he's being drawn out. We all go through seasons of difficulty that can cause us to lose sight of who we really are or to get out of touch with what we're feeling. God has a way of drawing us out, but that process can be painful. When we think about Meshech and Kedar* as a pair, we learn what God is drawing us out from. At the beginning of this journey, we're being pulled out of darkness toward the light. Alas! This too can be unwelcome at first (think about coming out of a dark movie theater on a sunny day).

The words that surround these places should bring us encouragement. We sojourn (stay temporarily) in the place of drawing out. The land of darkness is a tent city. Both of these ideas speak to this initial struggle as being impermanent. Indeed, being drawn out of whatever darkness we've been experiencing is temporary. It's just the starting point. The first steps and the first song to be sung at the very beginning of a long and meaningful journey. Although temporary, this starting point is also necessary. If you don't know where you're starting, it will be difficult to make it to the end.

*Hebrew poetry does not rhyme sounds (like Dr. Seuss) but, instead, rhymes ideas on parallel lines (parallelism). So Meshech and Kedar are certainly meant to be linked.

Lifeline: Prayer Journaling *(Prayer)*

Spend time today praying and journaling about your starting point. Discuss these questions with God:

Lord, are there ways that I've been holding back in my relationship with you? Why do you think I'm holding back?

Father, how is the turmoil of the world affecting my spirituality?

When I think about you "drawing me out" I feel...anxious, excited, free... Lord, how will you start drawing me out?

God, show me the darkness in my life. What first steps can I take to come into the light?

In a few sentences, describe your starting point:

Plan for Encounter: Have you secured a location for your personal retreat?

I lift up my eyes to the hills. From where does my help come? My help comes from the Lord, who made heaven and earth.
Psalm 121:1-2

Storyline: Read Psalm 121

There's something strange going on in the opening lines of this Psalm. I don't know about you, but when I look at the hills or gaze upon mountains, I feel inspired and closer to God. The Psalmist expresses the exact opposite. He looks to the hills and immediately needs a reminder that God is the only God; that God is the only creator and protector. What's going on with these hills?

If you've read through the Old Testament then you're probably familiar with idols like Baal, Asherah and others. In Israel, these foreign gods did not have temples. Instead, they were worshiped at "high places." That same impulse in us that causes us to worship the true God when we're inspired by nature, may have inspired idol worshipers to set up shop atop Israel's vistas. When you lifted up your eyes to the hills of Israel, you were seeing a panorama of idolatry.

In western society, the absence of idols on high places or street corners can fool us into thinking that idolatry is no longer a problem. It is true that we are not tempted with idolatry when we look at vast landscapes. Quite the opposite, we are more likely to be tempted when we stare at tiny screens. We've moved from gods on the peaks to gods in our pockets.

If we use the Psalmist's response to define idolatry, we may be able to get a better handle on the depths of false worship in our lives. Our idols don't need names like Baal to impact our lives. Is anything in your life causing you to...

...seek comfort from unhealthy sources that are not God? (v1-2)
...question if God really cares and is attentive to you? (v3-4)
...live a different life depending on your environment? (v5-6)
...be tempted by evil and feel helpless to overcome? (v7-8)

It is challenging to encounter God if we're filling our lives with gods that are not gods at all. The first step is to make a search of the hill country and identify the idols. We will find it difficult to make it to the mountaintop if we can't get our eyes off the hills (or our screens).

Lifeline: Limit Technology *(Fasting)*

Consider the following:
How do you seek comfort from sources that aren't God?

Have you been wondering if God really cares about you?

Are you the same person at work, school, home and church?

Do you feel constantly tempted? Do you feel powerless to overcome?

This might not make sense until you try it, but your smartphone (or other screens) might be the source of any negative answers you may have had to the questions above. Social scientists have been sounding alarms for years that smartphones are addictive, cause depression and anxiety, hurt relationships, promote secret (sinful) activity, and more. If there is idolatry in your life, chances are, your smartphone is the "high place" where the idols are making their stand. Smartphones have become such an integral part of our lives that some have theorized that we are living in a new era of humanity: The Augmented Era. Our technology is more than just a tool. It's a part of us. It's unrealistic to go back to the 1990's and get rid of our phones. Instead, we can intentionally practice healthy limits. Even the smallest change will give the idols less power, and God more room, to impact your life.

Ideas:
Put your phone out of sight instead of in your pocket when you are at home.
Turn your phone off for a set time each day.
Stop using your phone in bed.

It may be wise to meditate, pray, and seek advice from people close to you as you seek to set a limit.

For the next 29 days I will limit my smartphone use by:

Plan for Encounter: Think ahead about ways you can limit contact but still be reached while you are away.

Pray for the peace of Jerusalem!
May they be secure who love you!
Peace be within your walls
and security within your towers!
Psalm 122:6-7

Storyline: Read Psalm 122

The worshipers on their way to encounter God on Mount Zion would not have been able to check twitter to get the latest news about Jerusalem. If the city was in turmoil from war, division, or drought, their worship would be jeopardized. So, early in their journey, they cried out in prayer for the peace of Jerusalem.

Have you ever tried to worship God when you're stressed out? How hard is it to focus on what you're reading in the Bible when your head is swimming with anxiety? We need peace if we're going to encounter God. If our outer lives or our inner souls are in turmoil, we may miss out on the presence of God despite the planning and preparation of these devotionals.

In verses 6-8, David* pens a poetic masterclass on peace. He focuses on three aspects that we would do well to examine. Each perspective on peace is also echoed and expanded upon by David's great descendant, Jesus, in the Sermon on the Mount.

Peace within your walls
This is inner peace. This is quieting the noise of the world around us and finding peace within ourselves. Our circumstances are often chaotic and outside of our control. But that does not mean we are helpless. Jesus promises blessing for those who keep their hearts pure. They will see God. (Matthew 5:8)

Security within your towers
The towers of Jerusalem looked out from the city to the surrounding country. While many things are outside of our control, like a tower guard, we can control what we let into our lives. Jesus calls this having a good eye. (Matthew 6:22-23)

For my brothers and companions' sake
David looks beyond his own peace and considers the security of his friends and family. So much of our peace depends on our relationships. It's nearly impossible to find security in God when our relationships are in turmoil. Jesus would urge us to leave our gift at the altar and go make peace with our brother. (Matthew 5:23-24)

*Psalms attributed to specific authors may have been written by the person named or written in the style of the person named.

Lifeline: Listen for Peace *(Meditation)*

The prompts below will help you spend imaginative time listening to God. There's no need to rush. Approach each exercise with patience and write down your reflections.

Imagine yourself as a city with a strong wall around it. Everything outside the city fades away and all you can see is what's happening inside. Where do you see turmoil within the walls? What thoughts or emotions are regularly causing you to feel anxious or insecure?

Take a moment to journal your experience:

Next, imagine you are high up in a guard tower. Outside the wall, there are many things trying to get inside and cause chaos. Close your eyes and imagine them. Think about your life. What sources of stress and anxiety have broken through your walls and made it to your heart, mind, and body? What would it be like if those things were dealt with or removed?

Take a moment to journal your experience:

Now, think about your "citizens" (family, friends, brothers and sisters in Christ), anyone that you regularly interact with. Take a moment to picture individual faces and pay attention to how you feel. Is there anyone who causes you to feel anxious? Are there relationships where you feel insecure? Do you have unresolved tension in your heart?

Take a moment to journal your experience:

Lastly, pray for the peace of your Jerusalem. Ask God to give you the heart of a peacemaker. (Matthew 5:9) Going into the Encounter with a greater sense of peace will allow greater connection with God.

Plan for Encounter: You may want a special notebook & pen to journal your experience.

Have mercy upon us, O Lord, have mercy upon us, For we have had more than enough of contempt.

Psalm 123:3

Storyline: Read Psalm 123

God is cheering for you! He's your biggest fan. In fact, he wants the very best for all of his people, so he takes a gracious disposition toward us. God's posture toward his people can be described with one word: Grace – and it truly is amazing.

Because God is gracious, he shows us mercy. Mercy is not the same as grace even though we often use the words interchangeably. Here, the psalmist's cries for mercy are prayers for relief. Since we live in a world that does not honor God, we are unfortunately familiar with the weight of contempt and scorn that causes this Psalm's tone of distress.

As we climb toward an encounter with God, we are reminded by each Psalm we sing that the deep flaws of this world affect our souls. How can we stand up straight after our backs have been bowed by the weight of the world's despair?

We can ask God for the compassionate relief of His mercy. As this Psalm says, we are merely servants and maidservants looking to the hand of our master, knowing he alone has the power to grant us relief. The psalmist prays with the greatest vulnerability, "so our eyes look to the Lord our God, till he has mercy upon us." And then he begs for mercy.

As Christians, we can easily take God's mercy for granted since the relief that Jesus secured for us on the cross is so complete. Where this psalmist felt compelled to beg God, hoping he would grant mercy in the future, we have the privilege of looking back at the cross of Christ and knowing that God has acted with the utmost compassion.

This brief Psalm ends by mentioning those who are at ease or who show contempt (looking down on others) with their pride. The psalmist writes, "Our soul has had more than enough of" them. Interestingly, when we fail to understand the magnitude of mercy and become too at ease with grace, we can become like those that the Psalmist wants nothing to do with. The cross tells us that our master has granted mercy. May our hearts respond with ever-increasing gratitude for the grace of God. And when we feel crushed by the weight of the world, may we lift our eyes to the master of mercy.

Lifeline: Be Moved by Mercy *(Prayer Posture)*

We can shake up our prayer times by changing our postures, both spiritually and physically.

Psalm 123:1-3 paints a vivid picture of servants in need of mercy. Can you see their eyes lifted up toward their master, waiting patiently for him to grant mercy? Conversely, v. 4 causes us to imagine those who are at ease. Maybe you can envision such a person lounging without care.

Consider the posture of your life toward God. God does not want us to be insecure or tense in our relationship with him. But at the same time, we should not simply lounge around.

What is a posture that pleases God? This Psalm alludes to postures of dependence, humility, patience, and intimacy. Are these the ways that your spirit interacts with the Holy? Take a moment to write down how each of these postures could be lived out in your walk with God:

- Dependence -

- Humility -

- Patience -

- Intimacy -

Now, let's move from the spiritual to the physical in our posture. Some people love to pray while walking in the woods. Maybe you pray in your favorite chair or even in the car. Have you ever thought about how your physical posture during prayer affects your conversation with God? For example, prayer walks in the woods might result in overly casual or unfocused prayers. Today's lifeline is all about seeing our need for mercy as we approach God. Let's physically take on the posture of one seeking mercy from a greater power in prayer:

- ○ Find a private place where you can pray.
- ○ Read Romans 5:6-8 (out loud if possible).
- ○ Got on your knees if you are able.
- ○ Place your hands together with palms touching and fingers extended (like the emoji) instead of folding your fingers together.
- ○ Close your eyes and look up.
- ○ Talk to God about mercy in light of this passage in Romans. Thank him for showing you mercy because of his gracious posture toward you.

Plan for Encounter: Make necessary arrangements with your spouse, children, or roommates so you can retreat with less anxiety.

If it had not been the Lord who was on our side.
Psalm 124:1

Storyline: Read Psalm 124

The pilgrim's playlist is not as random as it may seem. Our last Psalm focused on grace and mercy. The natural reaction to such mercy is gratitude. Sure enough, our next prayer song is all about being thankful. Interestingly, the words thanks and gratitude are never mentioned. This Psalm hints at an appreciation that comes from a deeper place than a simple thank you might provide.

In the opening lines, we are urged to consider a profound truth: "If it had not been the Lord who was on our side." If the grace and mercy from Psalm 123 had not been God's character and disposition, where would we be? David, the Psalmist, recounts specific examples of God's gracious presence with great poetic skill. Angry people rose against him like raging waters in a storm. Predators flashed their sharp fangs. Traps were set. But with God at his side, David escaped all of them.

The last verse presents all of this as a universal truth: "Our help is in the name of the Lord, who made heaven and earth." There are two claims made here about the source of our help.

1) The name: We don't say "in the name of him or her" in our language today, so it may lack context when we read it in scripture. To say "in the name of" is to call upon the full essence of a person, their entire character. When you look at many of the great men and women of the Bible, their names had significant meaning for who they were and what they did. For example, Moses means drawn out. He was drawn out of the Nile as a baby, and he grew up to draw God's people out of Egypt. We often end our prayers by saying, "In the name of Jesus." We aren't merely referencing his name. We're calling on his character of grace and truth to hear and answer our prayers. So, when David says, "Our help is in the name of the Lord," he's saying that our help is in God's character. Because of who our God is, we can count on his help.

2) Who made heaven and earth: This claim is more straightforward. It is not a claim of character but a claim of power. Everything is God's. If He made it, He is fully able to protect us from anything in His creation that may come our way.

Are we living in the truth of these claims? Or are we doubting God's providence and protection? Deep gratitude may be the key to embracing the grace and mercy of God more fully.

Lifeline: Deep Gratitude *(Journaling)*

The creative journaling activity of writing a letter to God may help cultivate deeper gratitude.

Ponder the question posed by David in this Psalm: "If it had not been the Lord who was on our side," by writing a thank you note to God in the space below. It's easy to be thankful for the good things in our lives (and those things should be included), but this Psalm calls us to also consider the providence of God even in the most challenging moments of our lives.

Dear God,

Thank you...

Sincerely,

Reflect on your letter:
In what ways has the character (name) of God protected you?

How do you see his ultimate power over creation displayed?

Plan for Encounter: With 10 days to go, you can check the 10 day forecast and begin to think about the clothing and gear you'll need.

Those who trust in the Lord are like Mount Zion, which can never be moved, but abides forever.
Psalm 125:1

Storyline: Read Psalm 125

What shakes you? What knocks you off track or threatens to topple your faith? This Psalm begins with a bold proclamation about those who put their trust in the Lord; like Mount Zion, they cannot be moved.

If we imagine ourselves among a caravan of pilgrims journeying up to Jerusalem, maybe at this point we can see the mountains surrounding Jerusalem in the distance. We're struck by their beauty but also by their permanence. They reach up toward the heavens, while at the same time, they are firmly rooted deep in the earth. There are a couple of lessons we can learn about our security in God from this prayer song.

First, the truth is mountains can move, both spiritually and physically. Spiritually, Jesus uses hyperbole to explain that the faithful can move mountains. Physically, all mountains are slowly being eroded. Mountains in Michigan's Upper Peninsula are some of the oldest mountains on earth and have been worn down to glorified hills. But this Psalm is not just referencing any mountain. It's referencing Mount Zion, the temple mount on which the Holy of Holies housed the presence of God. This mountain cannot be moved. Even though the temple no longer rests on Mount Zion, God's presence remains unshakeable in the lives of those who trust in Him.

Secondly, this Psalm uses the mountains that surround Mount Zion and Jerusalem to illustrate how God protects us. What greater protection than to be hemmed in by mountains? We would do well to not only examine if we have put our trust in the Lord/Mount Zion but also to examine what we're surrounding ourselves with. In what ways do you see yourself dwelling securely, encompassed and surrounded by God and the things of God? In what ways might you be open to attacks on your faith? What things or people are threatening to rob you of security?

Lifeline: Security Check *(Prayer Journal and Posture)*

Just like large companies or individual households, it's important for us to check our security systems from time to time.

Surrounded:
Begin this exercise by closing your eyes and picturing your surroundings. Not your physical surroundings but your relationships, career, hobbies, and the like. You could use your calendar from last week as a reference point. What's in your orbit? As you pray and picture each thing, ponder, is this something that brings me security in God or leaves me vulnerable to attack? Take a moment after your prayer to write down what God puts on your heart.

Secured:
Now take the focus of your prayer from your surroundings to yourself and your relationship with God. Are you secure in God? Do you feel deeply rooted like a mountain? Do you feel confident to reach out and up to God, or is there fear or distance? Ask God what might be stealing your security. After your prayer, write down what God puts on your heart.

Like Mount Zion:
Lastly, combine what the Spirit has placed on your heart by praying in a new physical posture. Stand before God with confidence. Keep your arms by your side and simply look up. As you gaze heavenward, pay attention to your feet planted firmly on the earth that God created. Talk to God about becoming a secure place for his Holy Spirit to dwell like Mount Zion by relying on him alone. Then, picture the mountains that surround you. Ask God to help you to only put your trust in the people and things that will keep your heart, mind, body and, soul secure in God.

Plan for Encounter: Your encounter will be a space for intimacy with God. You may want to pack a candle and matches.

We were like those who dream.
Psalm 126:1

Storyline: Read Psalm 126

Those who have established their security in the Lord (yesterday) are free to dream big. The context of this song establishes that our "pilgrim's playlist" was written or compiled after Israel's return from exile in Babylon. The first half of the Psalm details the emotions that accompanied Israel's restoration. Can you imagine the moment when some of the oldest Israelites once again set eyes upon the city they had been forced to leave seventy years earlier? Laughter and tears. Shouts of joy and praise. The renown, even amongst the other nations of their time. And perhaps most notably, the confidence to dream again.

The second half of this Psalm turns introspective. Even with the hopes of their nation restored, they are still struggling. Being a dreamer takes brave vulnerability. The exile narrative in scripture should increase our confidence to dream boldly and our trust to wait patiently.

On the surface, our hopes and dreams can seem ethereal. But the reality is that all dreams come from deficits. Who dreams for what they already have? A dream is an admission that something is missing. Hope is a plea for something unfulfilled. Like Israel, fresh out of exile, there are times when dreaming comes easy in our lives. Other times, as illustrated by the second half of this Psalm, we must dream through tears as we plant the smallest seeds of hope.

In either case, God is the one who can make our dreams a reality. He is the restorer of Israel, and one day he will be the restorer of all the earth. Paul tells us in Romans 8 that even the trees groan as they wait for this dream of restoration to be fulfilled. As we await this final reality, we can examine the smaller hopes and dreams that sit in our hearts. Do they line up with God's plan of restoration? If so, we can sing along with this Psalm of Ascent whether our "mouths are filled with laughter" or we "go out weeping." We can become like those who dream.

Lifeline: Dream Session *(Journaling Meditation)*

Our dreams could be placed into three categories: Fulfilled, unfulfilled, and broken. Spend time bravely reflecting and recording thoughts about your hopes and dreams.

Fulfilled
Like Israel crossing the sea and almost immediately complaining, we are often too quick to forget the prayers that God has answered in our lives. Unfortunately, it seems like we're wired to have long memories when it comes to disappointment and short memories when it comes to blessings. Take a moment to meditate. Can you identify five hopes, dreams, or answered prayers in your life? Write what God puts on your heart in the space below:

Unfulfilled
It's been said that God answers prayer in three ways: Yes, no, and not yet. Unfulfilled dreams fall into the not yet category. Proverbs 13:12 says, "Hope deferred makes the heart sick, but a desire fulfilled is a tree of life." Unfulfilled desires can be a great source of heartache in our lives. They can lead to bitterness. They can cause us to distrust God. (Of course, some of our dreams may not align with God's because of selfish or sinful thinking.) Meditate on "the wait." What are you still waiting on God to fulfill? Write down your deferred hopes and ponder what God may be planning as you continue to wait.

Broken
We'd risk denying reality if we talked about dreams and failed to mention the dreams that didn't work out. As human beings living in a fractured world, we will all experience the heartache of failed hopes in our lives. Relationships, ambitions, health, finances, and goals don't always work out, do they? It may be painful but revisiting our broken dreams with God is worth it. Have you ever spoken to God about the things that didn't work out? Often, we try to pray with the right words and tones. But it's also okay to "let God have it" when we're feeling pain. Take a moment to write down any broken dreams that you've faced, and then take your broken dreams to the One who's still waiting to see His dream of a restored world fulfilled.

Plan for Encounter: Speaking of dreams, it may be good to limit screen use and focus on getting rest so you can come into your retreat fresh.

Unless the Lord builds the house,
Those who build it labor in vain.
Psalm 127:1

Storyline: Read Psalm 127

The long journey up to Jerusalem must have given the pilgrims many opportunities to reflect upon their lives. Singing this Psalm raises an important question: What are we building? Like the journey to Jerusalem, your journey through the encounter experience allows you to pause and consider this question.

At any one time, we may be building careers, reputations, families, wealth, relationships, and most importantly, our relationship with God. Physical buildings take careful planning, attention to detail, and great skill to be erected successfully. The things that we're building in our lives are even more critical, but we often lack the wisdom, humility, and patience to see success. We can probably all look back and see a few things in our lives that ended up cobbled together instead of skillfully built.

The very first verse gives us all the instruction we need to build successfully: Let the Lord build it. Of course, we need to do much of the work ourselves, but just as a crew of workers is directed by a general contractor, we need to see our role as crew members, with God as the master builder. When those roles get confused, even our foundations can become shaky. Paul frequently used this illustration in his writings. To Corinth, he wrote, "No one can lay a foundation other than that which is laid, which is Jesus Christ." (1 Corinthians 3:11) To Ephesus, he wrote, "You are fellow citizens with the saints and members of the household of God, built on the foundation of the apostles and prophets, Christ Jesus himself being the cornerstone." (Ephesians 2:19-20) Jesus even calls himself the cornerstone in the gospels and rebukes the Jewish leaders for rejecting him as the new foundation of their faith.

Unfortunately, this Psalm about building has an ironic twist. It's the only Psalm of Ascents penned by Solomon. In one sense, Solomon was Israel's greatest builder. He built the king's palace and the temple in Jerusalem. But he was also a terrible builder. His family and faith crumbled late in his life because he began to follow his plan instead of building the way God desired. As you are preparing for an encounter with God, let this time provide an opportunity to reflect on your relationship. How would you evaluate your surrender to God's leadership and your partnership with Him?

Lifeline: Blueprint *(Searching Prayer)*

We probably spend a lot of time in our prayers asking God for things like wisdom and direction. How much time do spend listening for the answer? This exercise will help you ask questions and listen to God's response.

In the Luke 14:28-30, Jesus compares our relationship with God to a building project. We are urged to build wisely by sitting down and considering if we have what it takes to complete the work. Maybe this is something you did before committing your life to Christ. Interestingly, Jesus urges us to consider how we build after we have "laid a foundation."

What are you building with God?
Imagine coming into the encounter with the heart of a builder. The foundation of faith is laid and now it's time to build upward. What are some areas of faith that need to be strengthened, expanded, or even torn down? Meditate and write down what the Spirit offers:

Take your "building projects" into a searching prayer. Lay out each area before God and ask how He wants you to build with Him. After each request, pause and listen for a minute or so. Push through discomfort and try to keep your mind from wandering. Stay focused and listen until you feel like you have an answer from God.

Write down any insights as they come to you:

Look over your answers.
How did God speak to you? Write down a building project you'd like to bring into the encounter. When you meet God on the mountain next week there will be ample opportunity to revisit this in a safe and constructive environment.

Plan for Encounter: In one week you'll begin your encounter with God. Breathe deep and picture those first moments of retreat.

You shall eat the fruit of the labor of your hands;
You shall be blessed, and it shall be well with you.
Psalm 128:2

Storyline: Read Psalm 128

The flow of the pilgrim's playlist is divine. As we travel to Zion, we go from a song about building with God to a song about enjoying the fruits of our labor. Just as Jonathan ate the honey (1 Samuel 14), God wants us to experience the joyful results of laboring for him. He wants us to "eat the fruit of our labor," not just in the life to come but here and now. How encouraging to know that when we work for God and build with God, we get to "taste and see that the Lord is good." He wants our hearts and our happiness!

The economy of the ancient world revolved around the family. These lyrics praising wife and children are representative of the greatest possible success and blessing in that society. While we must avoid the oversimplified and false "health and wealth" gospel, we should see tangible signs of blessing in our lives when we fear (respect) the Lord and walk in his ways (obey). Too often, our Christian walk is more of a funeral march, when Jesus, instead, repeatedly connects the Christian life to a wedding. In fact, the only time Jesus goes to a funeral, he raises the dead. (John 11). He promises his disciples that whatever they give up for him, they will receive back multiplied, in this life and in the life to come. (Mark 10:30) Again, this isn't a direct formula for worldly wealth, nor should those who are struggling be looked at as unspiritual. This whole Psalm and its surrounding spiritual concept speak more to a mood than anything tangible. Do our hearts reflect fruitful abundance, or are we drifting through life as if we are not blessed beyond measure?

Too often, we take on the persona of the curmudgeonly Christian. Where in scripture do we see faithful and fruitful people wearing frowns? What's your mood? Do you emanate an atmosphere of happiness, or are you hobbling around in the humdrum? There are certainly times when we face trouble and hardship, even at a soul level, just as Jesus did, and as we'll see in the next Psalm. Are you letting those moments of struggle define your existence, or are you living in the blessed (happy) harvest of a life built on God? If you're more grumpy than grateful, examining your heart and counting your blessings may be wise.

Lifeline: Fruit Picking *(Prayer of Examination)*

Engage with the Spirit to examine the atmosphere you produce through this innovative approach to praying through scripture.

In Galatians 5:22-23, we learn that a life lived with God's Spirit produces fruit. Unlike the tangible (Hebraic-minded) illustrations of fruit that we see in Psalm 128, Paul illustrates the fruits of the Spirit with (Greek-minded) abstract character traits. A fruitful life is not so much measured in money or mansions but in mood and impact.

Pray through each fruit of the Spirit by quietly repeating the word over and over and thinking about your life/mood/atmosphere. Listen for the Spirit to show you what you are projecting to the world with each of these fruits. After you feel like you have an answer, write down what you could do differently to live an abundantly fruitful life in each area.

Love-

Joy-

Peace-

Patience-

Kindness-

Goodness-

Faithfulness-

Gentleness-

Self-control-

Look over the results of your prayer of examination. In what ways are you best displaying the fruitful life you've been blessed with in Christ? In what ways do you need to rely on the Spirit to bear greater fruit?

Plan for Encounter: Scout out the area where you have planned your retreat. Take note of trails, beaches, or vistas that might inspire you.

Greatly have they afflicted me from my youth,
Yet they have not prevailed against me.
Psalm 129:2

Storyline: Read Psalm 129

We are at war. This Psalm, more than any of the other Psalms of Ascents, high-lights the battle that God's people face. The honesty of the Bible is striking. Even as we ascend to worship and encounter God, we must admit that we are often in the fight of our lives. The lyrics to this Psalm speak to the battle in ways that line up with scientists' views about how our brains work.

The Psalmist pictures the pain that has afflicted him since his youth as plow lines down his back with "furrows long." This is a vivid illustration of an unknown af-fliction that he has suffered. It also accurately depicts what happens in our brains when we struggle with persistent temptation or addiction. It is believed that our brains are shaped like trenches being dug and well-worn paths being formed when we engage in repeated negative behaviors. Unfortunately, these long fur-rows plowed into our brains when we give in to sin only make it that much more difficult to overcome the next time we are tempted. Have "the plowers plowed upon your back, making long their furrows?" What temptations have you strug-gled with? Are you wrestling with addiction in your life?

Not only does this Psalm identify our struggle with temptation/addiction in a way that lines up with neuroscience, but it also offers an equally scientific solution. The Psalmist prays against his enemies and asks that they be like grass on the housetops. That may not sound very scientific, but with some imagination, it will. The thatched roofs of Judean homes would allow seeds dropped from birds to grow shallow roots in an undernourished environment. As the Psalmist continues, he remarks that the reaper and binder will never find a harvest up there. This is a poetic picture of how we can fight against the deep roots that temptation and addiction want to dig. We must starve them and not let them grow. We must cut them off before they can take root and dig furrows in our hearts and minds. Jesus uses hyperbole in the Sermon on the Mount to speak similarly, "If your right eye causes you to sin, tear it out."

Temptation, sin, and addiction can be great sources of heartache, shame, and struggle. But there is hope in God. Besides being offered solutions that work, we're given abounding grace and unending hope. No matter how difficult your battle, you can sing with this Psalmist, "Greatly have they afflicted me...yet they have not prevailed.

Lifeline: The Lord's Prayer *(Confession)*

Journey into prayer with Jesus and his disciples and experience the power of vulnerability that Jesus desired for his followers.

The Lord's Prayer *(Luke 11:1-4)* may be one of the most repeated paragraphs in the history of the world. It may also be one of the most misunderstood. Jesus certainly did not intend for his disciples to mindlessly repeat a prayer (or anything for that matter). Unfortunately, because this prayer is misused in some religious traditions, it is often ignored altogether in others. However, if we see the Lord's Prayer as an outline, with each line serving as a springboard into deeper prayer, we can use it as a template to connect with God in new ways. Spend a minute or two reading and praying about each prompt, and experience the intimate prayer that Jesus provided his followers:

Father, hallowed be your name- Begin your prayer time by putting God in his place (He's our Father and He's holy) and putting yourself in your place (You're His child). Spend time praising God.

Your kingdom come- Next, ask God for the kingdom to come. Pray about people in your life, saved or unsaved, who need kingdom perspective (i.e., to recognize the Lordship of Christ). Pray also, for a greater vision of God's kingdom to come to you.

Give us each day our daily bread- Think through what you need and ask God for it. This is where vulnerability gets turned up in this prayer. Without God's providence, we wouldn't even have daily sustenance.

And forgive us our sins- Now we're really getting vulnerable. Jesus wanted his followers to often think about their own sinfulness and to confess and ask for forgiveness. This cuts the grass off the roof before it gets to grow (see above).

For we ourselves forgive everyone who is indebted to us- We often try not to think about the people who've hurt us. Counterintuitively, Jesus instructs us to regularly consider those who've sinned against us and to forgive them. This painful and vulnerable habit keeps us from growing bitter roots and is a salve for relationships. He is a safe place to bring your hurt.

And lead us not into temptation- Lastly, and most vulnerable of all, Jesus wants us to not just think of how we've sinned but how we are inclined to sin. Ask Him to lead you away from temptation/addiction/sin.

Do you see that the Lord's Prayer has great power to bring you into an intimate and vulnerable conversation with God? It's not to be repeated mindlessly or ignored. It's a script we should return to whenever we struggle to find words for our prayers or feel stuck in our walk with God. How was your experience?

But with you there is forgiveness.
Psalm 130:4

Storyline: Read Psalm 130

In yesterday's Psalm and devotional, we dove deep into temptation, sin, and addiction. Then we prayed through the Lord's Prayer and asked for forgiveness. This is such a natural progression (to understand our sinfulness and then cry out to God for forgiveness) that Psalms 129 and 130 follow that same pattern. Having confronted our temptation and sinful nature, we now lift our voices "out of the depths" to sing about steadfast love, forgiveness, and redemption.

Our salvation is so sweet that it can be difficult for us not to take forgiveness for granted. So, imagine this: what if you lived in a world where every mistake you ever made was held against you with no real path to make things right? This is the reality that the pilgrims singing these songs lived in. The fact that they were journeying to Jerusalem meant that they were participating in the sacrificial system that foreshadowed our redemption. This system, divinely ordained by God, worked to alleviate some of the burdens of sin but could never fully atone (make peace). More than anything, it served to highlight just how sinful we are (Romans 7:7-12). As Israel followed the law century after century, their longing for a messiah (anointed savior) who could redeem them once and for all grew and grew. Even this Psalm reflects the longing of a people that desired a salvation that was promised but not yet delivered. "I wait for the Lord, my soul waits, and in his word I hope; my soul waits for the Lord more than watchmen for the morning... O Israel, hope in the Lord! He will redeem Israel."

We can almost feel their desperation and desire for a redeemer. And yet, generation after generation, their desire went unfulfilled despite passionate pleas to God like this Psalm. How blessed are we to be able to look back and praise God for the forgiveness that they longed for? What if our intensity as we praised and thanked God for his forgiveness matched the intensity of our spiritual ancestors when they begged for salvation? Jesus' death and resurrection entered us into a new epoch. He changed the direction of our gaze. He put redemption in the rear view mirror of world history. But that doesn't mean we have nothing to look forward to or even long for. We have redemption, but we still long for restoration. Our sin no longer counts against us. But our sin is not without effect. We still suffer its consequences every day. We see the decay that sin causes in our lives and in our world. As our ancestors begged God intensely for redemption, we would do well to long for the next epoch: the restoration He promised will come in His good and perfect timing.

Lifeline: Restoration Movement *(Scripture Reflection)*

Romans chapter 8 is considered by many to be the greatest chapter in the whole Bible, and it's all about the restoration to come. This reading exercise will help you read Paul's masterpiece on restoration and be moved by the Spirit in new ways.

Read Romans 8:1-39 slowly, from start to finish, out loud (if possible). If you are short on time, just choose one or two paragraphs to read.

Now read it again in the same way but pause for a few seconds after each verse. Use the space below to write down words or phrases that stand out to you or inspire you:

Next, look over the words and phrases that you wrote down. Read each one slowly and out loud, and then talk with God (pray) about why you wrote that phrase down or any questions you may have.

Lastly, read through Romans 8 one more time slowly, out loud, and see how it impacts you differently after doing this exercise.

What did you notice from this experience? How did it move you?

Plan for Encounter: Scout out the area where you have planned your retreat. Are there any coffee shops, cafes, or picnic areas you want to check out?

I do not occupy myself with things too great and too marvelous for me.
Psalm 131:1b

Storyline: Read Psalm 131

Have you ever connected restfulness with humility? Or restlessness with pride? When we lack peace or feel anxious, we often blame things like busyness, relational strife, or even chemical imbalances in our brains. All those things can certainly contribute to stress, but this Psalm introduces the possibility of a deeper source.

Written by David, this prayer song begins with a declaration of humility. The king keeps his heart and eyes low. He decides not to dwell on things that are beyond his understanding, however great or marvelous they may be. Then he directly connects this humble posture to a calm and quiet spirit. The word picture is beautiful: instead of occupying himself with the grandiose, he's trained his soul like a weaned child. Thus, not only is humility connected with restfulness, but it is also connected with maturity. An un-weaned child (baby) is "wanty" and never satisfied, always wanting more and seldom content. We might think that it is "grownup" behavior to demand clear answers to all of our questions and refuse to be satisfied. We might justify criticalness in our hearts as having high expectations. But do we ever pause to think what such a posture is doing to our souls? Israel's greatest leader and king would challenge us to choose the maturity of humble trust in God. He would call us to the rare combination of being childlike and content. He would implore us to put our "hope in the Lord from this time and forevermore."

We are only a few Psalms from Mount Zion. We are only a few days from our encounter with God. It's easy to see why this song needs to be sung and applied to our hearts. When we meet God, any posture other than humility will diminish our experience. Is your soul quiet and calm? Or is there a restlessness in your spirit? Now is the time to examine what the source of that restlessness may be. Now is the time to put your hope in the Lord.

Lifeline: The Rest of God *(Silence)*

The most uncomfortable part of your upcoming spiritual retreat might be silence. This practice session will help acclimatize you to silence and stillness.

Silence can be scary. We rarely have an opportunity to experience it. And most of us probably wouldn't call it an "opportunity." So much of our lives are filled with noise, images, and clutter. In our church services, the moments where there could be silent reflection are often "soothed" by peaceful background music. Our aversion to quiet even shows up in our language in the phrase "uncomfortable silence." Today's Psalm should cause us to wonder if we wouldn't find more peace in our lives if we embraced quiet. In the very beginning of scripture, God creates our world by breaking silence. Creation has been noisy ever since. But on the seventh day, He rested from His creative work. Since that work was done through speech, "and God said...," what if even God rested in silence? Jesus would later reveal that this Sabbath rest was for us to set an example that we would also seek out intentional rest. When we let our lives get too noisy, we miss out on parts of our great God, who is known to communicate through a "gentle whisper." When we rest in God, we are opened up to the rest of God.

Can you spend time in silence? Turn off your phone. Take a walk without headphones. Sit by the water or in a park. Get away and don't say a word. No need to even pray silently. Just listen to your thoughts. Listen for God whispering out from the Spirit inside of you. If you're super tired and fall asleep, that's okay too. Silence and stillness may be the toughest challenge of all for some of us. You decide the duration. Can you make it 5 minutes? A half-hour? More?

When you've finished, use the space below to reflect on your time of silence. Did you notice anything about the rest of God as you rested in God?

Plan for Encounter: Pack a spiritual book that you're working through or wanting to start. You'll have time in between activities to read.

**This is my resting place forever;
Here I will dwell, for I have desired it.**
Psalm 132:14

Storyline: Read Psalm 132

In the longest of the Songs of Ascents, we find three "passion plays." In the first, as the Psalm begins, we learn of David's strong desire to build a dwelling place for the Lord. He refuses to go into his own house, sleep in his own bed, or sleep at all until the temple is built. (See 2 Samuel 7) Despite his desire, God rejects David's request to build the temple because he has shed too much blood in his life. David passes his passion onto the next generation, and his son Solomon builds the temple on Mount Zion that we've been journeying toward over these last 13 days. Like the Israelites of verses 6-7, we've responded to the call, "Let us go to his dwelling place; let us worship at his footstool!"

After those verses, we enter the second passion play. God himself is called to arise and go to the temple. We are not just going to some religious place or experience. We are going to meet God! Amazingly, we find that God is even more passionate than David about his dwelling place. Being reminded of his oath to keep one of David's descendants forever enthroned, God declares, "This is my resting place forever, here I will dwell, for I have desired it." We often bring our desires to God, and we should. But have you ever thought of God's desires? Ultimately, he desires us. He wants to be with us, passionately, eternally. He found ways to be present among us in the past through the pillar of cloud and fire, through the temple, and through the word of His prophets. God is passionate and active in His desire to dwell with us.

Ultimately, this passion is fulfilled in Jesus, who stars in the third passion play of this Psalm. On the surface, Jesus' presence in this Psalm may not be obvious. But he shows up in a couple of ways. First, he's the fulfillment of God's promise to David that there would always be a descendant on the throne of Israel. Second, he's the living expression of the passion of God to do anything to dwell with his people. The very word "passion" comes from the Latin passio, which means to suffer. Passion is not fleeting desire or infatuation. Passion is proven by a willingness to suffer for that which you love. This is why we call the last week of Jesus' life the passion week and the last chapters of Matthew the passion account. Jesus, as God's perfect representative, shows us the passion of God by willingly suffering on the cross so God could dwell with his people once again and forevermore.

Lifeline: House Inspection *(Journaling)*

In Ephesians 2, Paul calls us "members of the household of God...being built together into a dwelling place for the Holy Spirit." In the devotional, we saw that David, God, and Jesus were passionate about building intimate dwelling spaces. Like hosts expecting honored guests, we would do well to examine the state of our dwellings. This journaling exercise will take you on a tour of the Holy Spirit's living conditions. Imagine your spiritual life as a home. Pray and take notes as prompted:

Welcome Mat and Entryway – Have you ever been to a home and felt totally welcomed right away? How open are you to the Spirit in your life? Is your door always open, or are you nervous about letting the spirit in?

Living Room – The living room is where life happens. Often, we separate our spiritual life from the rest of our lives too much. Is the Spirit a part of your whole life? Do you talk about God with your spouse, children, or roommates?

Dining Room – In many homes, the deep talks happen at the dinner table. Life with the Spirit is difficult. We need deep relationships with other spiritual people. When was the last time you had a good talk about God with a trusted friend?

Kitchen – If you have a well-stocked fridge, you can create delightful dishes for family and friends. Likewise, a person who interacts with God regularly can use the word for many things (2 Timothy 3:16-17). What delicious and nutritious fruit is your walk with God bearing? Is it time to restock the fridge with books, resources, or prayer partners that will add quality and variety to your walk with God?

Bedroom – Let's go there. The bedroom is the place of intimacy. Some Christians have the Spirit dwelling inside them but are content to sleep in separate beds. Is there coldness or distance in your relationship with God? Did something happen that needs to be worked out? If we've withdrawn, we may need to go through conflict to return to intimacy. Are you willing to hash it out so you can be near God again?

Plan for Encounter: Have you thought through everything you need to bring to be comfortable? Bedding, snacks, shoes, clothing, etc.

Behold, how good and pleasant it is when brothers dwell in unity.

Psalm 133:1

Storyline: Read Psalm 133

We don't go up to the temple alone. Even as we are on the cusp of a personal retreat with God, we are never truly solo. Over these two weeks of devotionals, you've interacted with countless people who've shaped you. You'll carry your relationships with you into your private retreat, even as you try to leave the world behind and focus on the Lord. And after your encounter, you'll descend back into the world and its people. The placement of this Psalm in the pilgrim's playlist is no accident. At festivals, up to a million people would pack Jerusalem. Dealing with God meant dealing with people, just as it does today. And so, as a penultimate focus, the Songs of Ascents wrap up by reminding us that it is essential to value unity with people if we desire unity with God.

This Psalm pictures unity with two beautiful examples that we might miss without some context. First, unity is described as oil running down Aaron's beard and even soaking the collar of his priestly robe. You may be imagining a thick, oily beard right now, and you're not only grossed out, but you're wondering what that has to do with unity. Priests were anointed with oil so they could serve at the temple, God's dwelling place. David illustrates that living in harmony with brothers and sisters is an anointing. It makes us like priests who are ready to serve God as he dwells among us. If you've had relational strife (and who hasn't?), then you know how it depletes your effectiveness for God. Unity makes us ready to serve.

The second example may remind us of a certain highly caffeinated soft drink, but it is actually a geography lesson. Mount Hermon is located in the far north of Israel, and at almost 10,000 feet (2,800 meters), it has a snowy peak. Not what we would expect for a mountain in the Middle East. Mount Zion, the temple mount in Jerusalem, on the other hand, is at a lower elevation and on the outskirts of a dry wilderness. David is saying that unity with one another is like snow falling in the desert. It's refreshing and invigorating. If your walk with God is dried up or you're feeling parched, examine your relationships. Have divisions, criticalness, attitudes, or hurts caused your relationships to be wrecked when they're supposed to be refreshing?

The Psalm ends by declaring that this kind of united temple worship is a commanded blessing. God demands that we do our part to have happy relationships in this life that will stretch even into eternity.

Lifeline: State of The Union *(Prayer Journaling)*

Examine the state of the relationships in your life by praying and journaling through the prompts below. If we do this work ahead of time, God can create more life-giving personal relationships when we return.

Directions: Listen for the Spirit. Under each category, write a few names that fit. Ask God to show you each individual at their very best. Pray a prayer of blessing and goodness over each person.

Family
-
-
-

Close Friends
-
-
-

Co-workers/Classmates
-
-
-

Hurting People
-
-

Lost People
-
-

Troubling Relationships (This might be the most challenging prayer and positive visualization but also the most rewarding.)
-
-

Challenge: Pay attention the next time you interact with each person. How does your prayer of blessing over them impact your relationship?

Come, bless the Lord, all you servants of the Lord,
who stand by night in the house of the Lord!
Lift up your hands to the holy place and bless the Lord!
May the Lord bless you from Zion,
he who made heaven and earth!
Psalm 134:1-3

Storyline: Read Psalm 134

We've arrived at the temple mount! The pilgrim's playlist has accompanied us on our ascent to Jerusalem and prepared our hearts to encounter God. How fitting that the last Psalm is a simple song of praise. But, when we look closely, maybe it's not so simple.

Of course, we want praise to be simple. On Sunday mornings, we might wake up with a vision of a happy family effortlessly piling into the car to attend a church with no problems and then coming home refreshed and ready for the week. But how often is that our experience?

One phrase in this Psalm hints that the pilgrims' arrival at Mount Zion is not without some struggle. "All you servants of the Lord, who stand by night." It appears as if they've arrived at night. Maybe they pushed hard on the last day of travel, hoping to arrive before nightfall and secure lodging but were delayed. Whatever the reason, instead of arriving to the sounds and smells of active temple worship with its cacophony of timbrels and trumpets and the aromas of incense and sacrifice, they've arrived at a sleepy Mount Zion. Worship will have to wait. Or will it?

This last Psalm calls worshipers to bless the Lord even in the night. How have your plans for worship been interrupted in the last fifteen days? I imagine very few will arrive at this fifteenth devotional after fifteen days. We make plans, and life happens. Worship gets interrupted. One of the greatest skills we can develop as we mature in our faith is the ability to worship through interruptions. In multiple places in the Gospel of John, Jesus urges his disciples to walk in the light, not the dark. The dark is a place of stumbling and struggle. If we're honest, it's also a place where we often find ourselves. Maybe this is why Jesus speaks of it so frequently.

No matter when or how you got here, what matters most is that you got here. Whether you arrived after multiple stumbles or in the middle of a dark time, you're just a page-turn away from an encounter with God. Welcome to beautiful, beautiful Zion!

Lifeline: Preparing for Praise *(Reflection)*

Take some time before your upcoming encounter with God to reflect on the current postures of your heart.

Baggage: When we travel, we carry baggage. Traveling into this encounter with God is no different. As you head into a special time of praise, what baggage is weighing you down? Is there anything heavy on your heart?

Reflection: Take a moment to reflect on the last fifteen days. What lessons have you learned even before you experience your encounter with God?

Arrival: When we get to a new place, we are rarely at our best. On long flights, they even offer warm cloths so travelers can freshen up. What's happening in your life, emotions, and spirit as you reach the top of the mountain? Don't hold back as you journal about your current state of mind.

Expectation: Setting down in a new place is exciting and scary. As you think about your encounter with God, what are you expecting the experience to be like? What are you excited about? Is there anything you are anxious about?

Plan for Encounter: Your retreat begins tomorrow! Spend some time today making sure you have everything you need for the encounter.

Encounter

Personal Retreat with God

You've made it to the mountaintop.

Fifteen days of ascending to an encounter with God.
Readying your heart, mind, soul,
To worship at the temple,
To see his face.

Let two truths speak to you at this moment:

One

When you meet with God, after ascending to the temple mount, he is not scary, overbearing, judgmental, or angry. You look at the face of God, and you see the face of a friend. You get to spend time with your friend.

Two

You are not on a mountaintop. God, your friend, has come down to meet you right where you are.

Let those truths relieve any pressure you may be feeling as you begin your encounter. You may even want to whisper to yourself, "I'm meeting my friend right where I'm at."

When we make all the preparations for a retreat like this and do the heart work of the last fifteen days of ascent, we can begin to put impossible expectations on this time. God brought you here. He's ready to be with you. That's all.

I'm meeting my friend right where I'm at.

"On this mountain the Lord of hosts will make for all peoples
a feast of rich food, a feast of well-aged wine,
of rich food full of marrow, of aged wine well refined.
And he will swallow up on this mountain
the covering that is cast over all peoples,
the veil that is spread over all nations.
He will swallow up death forever;
and the Lord God will wipe away tears from all faces,
and the reproach of his people he will take away from all the earth, for the
Lord has spoken.
It will be said on that day,
"Behold, this is our God;
we have waited for him, that he might save us.
This is the Lord; we have waited for him;
let us be glad and rejoice in his salvation."
For the hand of the Lord will rest on this mountain..."

Isaiah 25:6-10a

A Feast with A Friend.

God's people used the imagery of passages like Isaiah 25 to shape their dreams of the coming Messiah and his kingdom. Here, the coming king celebrates victoriously with a grand feast. Take a moment to imagine this wondrous feast. Can you see the long table piled high with choice food and drink? Can you smell the aroma as your mouth begins to water?

There's more to this feast than the food. We are told that a veil will be lifted, death will be no more, our tears will be wiped away, and sin will be dealt with. This is what God's people waited centuries for. This is what you've journeyed toward during the fifteen devotionals of Ascent. God is here.

All four gospels detail the feast that Jesus had with his disciples on the night that he was betrayed. We know it as the Last Supper. This final meal on the Mount of Olives, is so important to John, in particular, that he spends five chapters (out of twenty-one) detailing the moment. The event begins with Jesus humbly washing his disciples' feet and announcing that he will be betrayed and denied. During the feast, Jesus tries to comfort his distraught disciples as he talks about the primacy of love and the coming of the Holy Spirit. He ends by praying for himself, his disciples, and the world (including you).

Begin your encounter by reading John chapters 13-17. (Or if that seems like too much, just read John 15:1-7) Try to picture yourself in the room. Read slowly. Visualize. Imagine. Pause as often as necessary to reflect. Read out loud if possible. Have dinner (or breakfast) with your friend Jesus.

Take a moment to write down what struck you about this feast on the Mount of Olives:

We want our last words to count. Jesus certainly delivers. Scholars have pointed out that this is one of many passages in the Bible that appears to be a "chiasm." Picture a pebble dropped into a clear pond. A chiasm looks like rings radiating from a center point. Did you notice how Jesus began the dinner (Chapter 13) by washing his disciples' feet and asking them to do likewise so they could stay united by humility? Then, he ends their time together by humbly praying for them to stay united. (Chapter 17) In chapters 14 and 16, Jesus talks about the coming of the Holy Spirit and the challenge the disciples will face because of the world. The center of it all seems to be John 15:1-17.

It would not be a stretch to view these chapters of John as the most important words in all of scripture since they are Jesus' last and longest teaching. Moreover, we could think of the center of the chiasm (John 15:1-17) as the most important part of these last words.

If we had to boil Jesus' teaching down to its most essential part, it might be this short sermon about vines, branches, love, and friendship.

Let's examine this central section of the sermon even further. In the first eight verses of John 15, Jesus draws us in with a beautiful parable about vines and branches, possibly during an after-dinner walk through a vineyard. We can't live in Christ or bear fruit without a life-giving connection to God. In verses 9-17, like any good preacher, he makes his illustration practical. He leaves no room for interpretation: We must abide in the love of Jesus. We are called to sacrificially love just as Jesus loved us. And then, he closes this most central of teachings with a personal touch. It's heartbreaking to picture him looking into the eyes of the eleven remaining disciples as he says, "You are my friends."

Jesus wanted to make sure his disciples knew that he considered them friends right before he died. So, possibly the most central and important message in scripture is this: You, disciple of Jesus, are God's friend. We are not given commands so we can serve a master, but rather, so we can become friends of God. That's the message of the great feast on the Mount of Olives.

This may be the most important message about friendship with God in the Bible, but it's not the first. The entirety of scripture could be summed up as God fighting to restore his broken relationship with us. In other passages, faith heroes are called friends of God, and individuals experience moments of intimacy that preview the deep relationship God desires with all of us.

Having read about this moment in the upper room and Jesus' heartfelt message of friendship, to begin your encounter, you'll move from this feast to other faithful friendship moments in scripture as you craft your personal retreat with God. Each encounter is displayed as a recipe card, so the friendship feast can be prolonged as you spend time interacting with the Word and the Spirit.

As incredible as it would have been to be at the last supper, even as an observer, we have an even greater feast to look forward to. The ultimate fulfillment of Isaiah 25 still looms on the horizon. John uses the language of Isaiah in the very last chapters of the Bible as he describes the restoration to come. When he tells us about the new Jerusalem coming down out of heaven as a bride (it's a wedding feast), he recalls Isaiah 25, telling us, "He will wipe away every tear from their eyes, and death will be no more." (Revelation 21:4) As you try the recipes in this encounter, you are not just imitating the intimate friendship feast of John 13-17. You are imagining the very last supper, the moment when our friendship with God will be restored as we're ushered into eternity. The encounter you are having now is merely a taste.

If that seems like a lot, just remember this:

"I'm meeting my friend right where I'm at."

Rules of Engagement:

"On this mountain the Lord of hosts will make for all peoples a feast of rich food, a feast of well-aged wine, of rich food full of marrow, of aged wine well refined."
Isaiah 25:6

Think of the following pages as recipe cards for a buffet with God. The feast can last for half a day, a whole day, or (ideally) two days with an overnight in between.

You can pick and choose the recipes for Encounter that appeal to you the most by browsing the summary on the menu and at the top of each "recipe card." In doing so, you'll create an experience with God unique to you alone.

After your encounter, you'll be able to share with others who've used this resource and compare the recipes they chose. It may be enlightening to see how their experience differed.

Suggestions:
- **Unplug:** Get away from regular life and turn off your phone as much as you are able.
- **Go slow:** Take your time with each activity. It doesn't matter how many recipes you complete. It matters that you try to connect with God in each moment.
- **Pace yourself:** Leave space between exercises and devotionals, and feel free to add your own flavors.
- **Be open-minded:** Not everything that you see on a cooking show might look tasty, but if you're interested in becoming better at your craft, you'll try new things.
- **Plan:** Each recipe has a time window that should help you as you plan out your encounter.
- **Journal:** There's a space to select your festal menu (the activities you plan) and ample space to write notes as you complete each recipe.
- **No regrets:** You can always come back and try anything you didn't get to at another time.
- **No worries:** If any of these practices make you feel uncomfortable, then by all means skip them. And be sure not to cast judgment in the way that others approach these recipes.

Festal Menu:

Here's a summary of each recipe for encounter and estimated duration. Go in any order. Mark the recipes you intend to try:

Recipes:

He Walked with God - Take a walk with God (1 Hour) p.49

Holy Hospitality - Have a refreshing meal with God (1-2 Hours) p.50

Standing on the Promises - Meditate on God's promises (1/2 Hour) p.51

Face to Face - Design and plan a personal tent of meeting (1/2 Hour) p.52

Be Still - Sit in silence (5 min. to ½ hour) p.53

After God's Heart - Pray to care about the things God cares about (15 minutes) p.54

Born For Adversity - Reflect and pray with gratitude about the trials God has brought you through (1/2 Hour) p.55

A Three-fold Cord - Examine God's role in your closest relationships (1/2 Hour) p. 56

What Are You Doing Here? - Examine your purpose in life (1/2 Hour) p.57

Find Your Rhythm - Look at the rhythms and rituals of your life (1/2 Hour) p.58

Take A Nap - If you're tired, rest (1-2 Hours) p.59

A Prayer of Examen - Try a new (classic) spiritual prayer technique (1/2 Hour) p.60

Lectio Divina - Try a new (ancient) spiritual reading technique (1/2 Hour) p. 61

Dessert: (Be sure to finish with this)

Set a Stone - Find a stone of remembrance. (1-2 Hours) p.62

Here are some recipes I'd like to try in the future:

Here are some recipes that friends from my faith community tried:

Recipe: He Walked with God

Take a walk with God

TIME FRAME
1 HOUR

INGREDIENTS

WALKING SHOES
OPEN MIND
TRAIL/SIDEWALK

"Enoch walked with God, and he was not (found), for God took him."
Genesis 5:24

This is a mysterious passage. Scholars have a multitude of theories about what happened to Enoch. The writer of Hebrews includes Enoch in the "Hall of Fame of Faith" in chapter 11. There, we learn that he did not see death and that he was taken by God because he pleased God. What did Enoch do that made God want him in heaven immediately? All we know is that he walked with God.

Take a walk with God.

Go slow.

What does a walk with God entail? It could be a prayer walk where you talk to God, but it doesn't have to be. You could walk in nature or a neighborhood. You could walk in silence. Try to observe God's creation. Maybe a sprawling forest or a grand shoreline will inspire you. Maybe a single leaf or a tiny insect will cause you to stand in awe of God. God's creation on your path can spark conversation with the Creator.

As you pay attention to nature, also pay attention to yourself. How are you feeling? What anxieties have you brought with you? Is there distance in your relationship with God?

Rather than praying a structured prayer, you can just talk to God about whatever feelings come up, just as you would on a walk with any other friend.

When you return from your Enoch walk, take a moment to write down some of the highlights from your time.

Recipe: Holy Hospitality

Have a Refreshing Meal with God

INGREDIENTS	TIME	
COFFEE SHOP, CAFE OR PACK A PICNIC BIBLE, PEN, NOTEBOOK	**1-2 HOURS**	

"Let a little water be brought, and wash your feet, and rest yourselves under the tree, while I bring a morsel of bread, that you may refresh yourselves, and after that you may pass on."
Genesis 18:4-5

Abraham is called a friend of God in multiple places throughout scripture. Here, he is visited at his sprawling tent-home under the shade of the oaks of Mamre by three mysterious figures. Some associate them with the Father, Son, and Holy Spirit, or Jesus and two angels.

Abraham seems to understand that these are no ordinary visitors. He bows to them and invites them to stay and have a meal. After they agree, he runs to his wife Sarah to urgently get the kitchen going. Without refrigeration, the bread had to be made fresh, the oven reheated, and the calf slaughtered and roasted. This was not a quick encounter.

One of the reasons Jesus gives for his friendship with his disciples in John 15 is, "I have called you friends, for all that I have heard from my Father I have made known to you." (John 15:15) Similarly, "the Lord" reveals intimate details about his plans with Abraham and Sarah during this meal. Sarah learns that she will have a child in a year's time and famously laughs at the news. After the meal the Lord said, 'Shall I hide from Abraham what I am about to do?'" (Genesis 18:17) He then reveals his plan to destroy Sodom and Gomorrah, which sends Abraham to his knees in intercessory prayer.

What might God reveal to you as you eat together? Practice listening as you eat. Feel free to pray, read, and dream.

At Oblate School of Theology, there is a table with a statue of Jesus sitting in one of the chairs. People can go and have lunch with "Jesus." Even with a physical representation of Jesus at the table it can still be difficult to remember his presence. God is present. Whatever effort you make during this meal to experience his presence will surely be worthwhile.

What did God reveal during your meal? Take a moment to write down impressions from the Spirit.

Recipe: Standing on the Promises

Meditate on God's Promises		
INGREDIENTS BIBLE NOTEBOOK PEN	**TIME** **1/2** HOUR	
"The friendship of the Lord is for those who fear him, and he makes known to them his covenant." Psalm 25:14		

Friends confide in each other. This is a common thread in passages about friendship in the Bible (Genesis 18:17, John 15:15). In scripture, God reveals himself through a series of promises known as covenants. It is incredible that God would ever promise anything to his fallen creation. But, in his grace, he enters into agreements with us and proves his faithfulness again and again. At the same time, we constantly prove our inability to be faithful to our side of the covenants. Even as we continually break our promises, God never breaks His!

Slowly read through and examine each covenant and write down what each promise means for you:

Genesis 2:15

Genesis 3:15

Genesis 6:7

Genesis 12:1-3

Leviticus 26

Deuteronomy 29-30

2 Samuel 7:12-16

Acts 2

Lastly, pray about the ways God has been faithful to you in your life. How has he fulfilled his promises to you?

Recipe: Face to Face

Design & Plan a Personal Tent of Meeting

INGREDIENTS	TIME	
NOTEBOOK **CREATIVITY**	**1/2** **HOUR**	

"Now Moses used to take the tent and pitch it outside camp, far off from the camp, and he called it the tent of meeting. And everyone who sought the Lord would go out to the tent of meeting...Thus the Lord used to speak to Moses face to face, as a man speaks to his friend."
Exodus 33:7, 11

We increasingly neglect the importance of place and space in our friendship with God. You can even see it in church architecture. Older church buildings are often some of the most beautiful landmarks in a city. Unfortunately, modern church buildings seem to value function over beauty. Take a moment to consider the space (time, place, atmosphere) where you regularly meet with God. It's okay if you don't have such a space yet.

Is there a space that you could set up as a tent of meeting for yourself?

This could be a room like a closet or even a corner. Or it could be a place like a park bench, tree, trail, or waterfront.

If you read more about Moses, you'll see that he was given blueprints from God for an even greater meeting space, the Tabernacle.

In the space below, write or sketch out a blueprint for your own personal tent of meeting.

Location:

Time/Frequency:

Atmosphere:

Special Details:

Recipe: Be Still

Sit in Silence

INGREDIENTS	TIME	
COMFORTABLE QUIET SPACE	**5 MINS TO 1/2 HOUR**	

"Fear not, stand firm, and see the salvation of the Lord, which he will work for you today. For the Egyptians whom you see today, you shall never see again. The Lord will fight for you, and you have only to be silent."
Exodus 14:13-14

Can you imagine how difficult it would have been for an Israelite to trust and be silent at this moment when they were hemmed in between the Egyptian army and the sea? Silence can be difficult for us even when we are not in such dire circumstances. We frequently seek to fill any dead air with noise, busyness, or distraction. We are tempted to take out our phones during even the shortest waits. We might need stillness and silence more than ever.

How long can you just sit and be still? Set a loose goal and go for it.

Being still doesn't mean you aren't doing anything. It's actually a lot of work, especially if we are not used to it. Here are some things you can focus on to get the most out of stillness and silence:

Notice your breath. Remember that we were created from the breath of God, and Jesus breathed his Spirit into his disciples.

Listen for God to speak to you. God has a way of getting thoughts through to us in moments when we can hear him.

Follow along with your thoughts. What do you find when you let yourself think without the influence of a screen or headphones?

Look around and observe. In our overstimulated world, we often miss the simple beauty that surrounds us wherever we are.

When your time is over, take a moment to write down your observations. How did you find this experience? Where did your thoughts keep going? Did God speak to you?

Pray to Care About the Things God Cares About	
INGREDIENTS BIBLE PRIVATE PLACE TO PRAY	**"The Lord has sought out a man after his own heart..."** 1 Samuel 13:14
TIME FRAME **15 MINS**	

David is never specifically called God's friend like Abraham and Moses are, but his intimacy with God is unrivaled. Moreover, David exemplified deep friendship in his relationship with Jonathan. Unlike Saul, David cared about God's heart. David aligned his priorities with God's priorities and his will with God's will. (Acts 13:22)

Does this describe your heart?

Spend a few minutes meditating or searching the scriptures. Write down three verses that point to what God values most:

Spend time praying to have a heart that wants what God wants. Write down anything that the Spirit brings to your awareness during your prayer:

Recipe: Born for Adversity

Reflect & Pray with Gratitude About the Things God has Brought You Through.

INGREDIENTS	TIME FRAME
GRACIOUS & OPEN HEART	1/2 HOUR

 "A friend loves at all times, and a brother is born for adversity."
Proverbs 17:17

This idealized description of friendship is both beautiful and impossible. No human friendship is all love all the time. And sometimes, instead of being born for adversity, our close relationships are the cause of adversity!

God's friendship with us is the exception. He never fails to love us. And he's willing and ready to be at our side through all adversity.

Take time to think through the times of adversity you've faced in your life. These may be inflicted by nature, people or even ourselves. How has God proven his unfailing love? How has Jesus been the ultimate brother in adversity? Use the space below to catalog praise and thanksgiving for each instance of God's love and fidelity:

Are there any areas in your life where you don't feel God's love? Are you currently facing adversity? Ask God to be the friend and brother that Proverbs 17:17 describes.

Recipe: A Three-fold Cord

Examine God's Role in Your Closest Relationships

INGREDIENTS	TIME	
A HEART FOR GOD & STRONG FRIENDSHIPS	**1/2 HOUR**	

"And though a man might prevail against one who is alone, two will withstand him – a three-fold cord is not quickly broken."
Ecclesiastes 4:12

Although this passage is often shared at weddings, Solomon is not specifically talking about marriages when shares the power of two over one. (But it certainly applies.) After poetically describing the benefits of two, he switches abruptly in the last verse to the even greater benefit of three.

From an engineering standpoint, when a third strand is added to a braid, it becomes exponentially stronger. The third strand that can strengthen any relationship is God. As you spend time alone with God, take this moment to think through your closest relationships: Spouse, children, friends, or the people you prayed for on day 14 of the Ascent.

Pray about each relationship and invite God into it. Write down ways that God could come in and strengthen each relationship that he puts on your heart in the space below:

Recipe: What Are You Doing Here?

Examine Your Purpose in Life		
INGREDIENTS PEN & OPEN POSTURE	**TIME** **1/2** HOUR	
"There he came to a cave and lodged in it. And behold, the word of the Lord came to him, and he said to him, 'What are you doing here, Elijah?'" 1 Kings 19:9		

This question from God is so good (and Elijah has such a hard time hearing it) that He asks it again a few verses later. You may have had the same thought as you began this personal retreat. What am I doing here? Hopefully, as you complete recipes in this feast with God, your friend, you'll understand the value of this time. God's question to Elijah was about more than the here and now. "What are you doing here?" is THE question, isn't it? What's my purpose? What was I born to do? What vision do I have for my life? Those are big questions that most of us probably try to avoid.

Let's put ourselves in Elijah's shoes and imagine that God is asking us the ultimate question: What are you doing here?

Pray, listen for God to whisper, search the scriptures, and beg God to show you what he wants your life to be. In the space below, write, draw, and dream the results of your prayer time.

An exercise like this can be intimidating. It was even for Elijah! Look at your results and write down one small step you can take right away:

Recipe: Find Your Rhythm

Look at the Rhythms & Rituals of Your Life		
INGREDIENTS CALENDAR & SCHEDULE	**TIME** **1/2** **HOUR**	
"These are the appointed feasts of the Lord that you shall proclaim as holy convocations; they are my appointed feasts." Leviticus 23:2		

The Hebrew people set the rhythms of their lives to the tune of God through a series of Holy Days that dominated each season of the year. Have you ever stopped to think about what the rhythms of your life are based upon? What is the last holiday (Holy Day) that you celebrated? Even the Christian holidays we celebrate have been hijacked by our increasingly secular society. It may be time to march to the beat of a different drum.

Take some time to answer these questions that can help reorient your rhythms and rituals:

You may be reading this in the middle of the summer, but we'll start with this: How can your celebration of Christian holidays (Christmas, Easter, etc.) be more Christian?

What are some rituals you could work into your life that would get you off the world's calendar and into a rhythm with God?

Daily: (Think devotional times)

Weekly: (Think times with other Christians)

Monthly: (Think special times with God)

Yearly: (Think special retreats with God)

Recipe: Take a Nap

If You're Tired, Rest.

INGREDIENTS	TIME FRAME
COMFORTABLE & QUIET PLACE	**1-2 HOURS**

 **"And he lay down and slept under a broom tree."**
1 Kings 19:5

Elijah came into his special encounter absolutely exhausted by recent events, increased activity, dealing with an unbelieving world, and emotional and spiritual stress. You might have come into this retreat feeling any or all of those stresses as well.

Elijah rested. He took a nap just like Jesus, and many other men and women in the Bible did. Sleeping might not have been a part of your plan, but if you need to rest, you should. Elijah was so tired he could not have seen or heard God until after resting. This might be true for you. The rest of the recipes and an amazing encounter with God, your friend, will be waiting for you when you wake up.

Try a New (Classic) Spiritual Prayer Technique

INGREDIENTS	TIME	
A QUIET SPACE & AN OPEN HEART	1/2 HOUR	

"Search me, O God, and know my heart! Try me and know my thoughts! And see if there be any grievous way in me, and lead me in the way everlasting."
Psalm 139:23-24

We often forget, or ignore, that we come from a rich heritage of Christians trying to encounter and build a friendship with God. If we're open to new things, one of the practices of old might just be the thing that makes our walk with God new!

Ignatius of Loyola developed and passed on this prayer technique that allows us to examine ourselves at the end of the day through a conversation with God, just like we would talk to a friend. Follow these steps into a new and intimate talk with God:

1. Invite God's presence into your prayer time. It might feel strange but try to imagine that he is with you. He is truly with you. And if he's not, then you are just talking to yourself, which is even more strange.
2. Think through your day with a posture of gratitude. "This is the day the Lord has made, let us rejoice and be glad in it." (Psalm 118:24)
3. As you review the day, identify one good thing (encouragement/consolation) and one bad thing (disappointment/desolation) that occurred.
4. Spend some time "praying into" the disappointment (desolation or shortcoming) that you experienced. Be real with God like you would talk to any friend. He can handle it.
5. Look forward to tomorrow with hope. Tell God what you are excited about. Share with God just like you would with a friend.

After you've completed the prayer of examen, take a moment to write down your thoughts about connecting to God in this way. Is this a kind of prayer you are likely to repeat? Why or why not?

Recipe: Lectio Divina

Try a New (Ancient) Spiritual Reading Technique	
INGREDIENTS **A BIBLE** **& AN OPEN HEART**	**"The Lord is my shepherd; I shall not want."** Psalm 23:1
TIME FRAME **1/2 HOUR**	

There are so many ancient Christian practices that have been forgotten, ignored, or misunderstood. One example is Lectio Divina or divine reading. We typically approach a text with a mindset of studying the text and gleaning insights for our minds. This is a great way to approach the Bible. But there are other ways that may speak to our hearts or even our souls. Lectio Divina is a way of reading that stirs our hearts and attempts to connect us with the Holy Spirit as we look over a text. Friendships require facts *and* feelings.

Follow this recipe to divinely read Psalm 23:
- Read Psalm 23 very slowly, pausing between lines & verses to reflect. Take a few moments after reading it to think about what you read.
- Did any words or phrases stick out to you?
- Now read the chapter again. Do not hurry through it. Read it out loud if possible.
- Did you hear something new? Did one of the ideas that struck you on the first reading stand out even more?
- Read Psalm 23 a third and final time, practicing the same skills of observation.

Write down a phrase that feels like it was planted in your heart from this text:

Take a moment to reflect on that phrase and then take it to God in prayer.

How was your experience with Lectio Divina? You can do this with any verse or passage in the Bible. Will you be adding this ancient practice to your relationship with God? Why or why not?

Find a Stone of Remembrance

INGREDIENTS	TIME FRAME
STONE & OPTIONAL PERMANENT MARKER	**1-2 HOURS**

 **"So these stones shall be to the people of Israel a memorial forever."**
Joshua 4:7

Throughout scripture, we see God's people commemorating mighty moments with God. Abraham built an altar everywhere he set up camp. Moses and Miriam broke into song and dance after the waters of the sea buried the Egyptian army. David arranged for the temple to be built on the spot where an angelic plague was stopped.

In Joshua 4:1-7, God instructs one man from each of the 12 tribes to gather a stone that they will leave in the Jordan River to commemorate their crossing on dry ground into the Promised Land. The stones were to be big: "a stone upon his shoulder." And the marker was to inspire future generations: "When your children come ask you, 'What do these stones mean to you?'"

The phrasing of the children's question is so important. It's not just "What does this mean?" But rather, "What does this mean to you?" Even though this was a shared national experience, each Israelite would find personal meaning when they reflected on what God did during this miraculous encounter.

This may be true for you as well. If you are using Encounter as a shared resource with your faith community, many rocks may be collected, but each one will have a unique meaning and story from this time of retreat.

Go out and look for a rock, a walking stick, or some trinket that you can bring home to remind you of your time away with God, your friend.

As you are searching, talk to God about what this time has meant to you.

It might also be worthwhile to set a stone somewhere around your place of personal retreat so you can come back and remember this special time or bring others to your place of encounter.

Lastly, if you have a marker, you could write down an idea or passage that you want to remember from this experience on your trinket.

Descent

15 Days After Your Encounter

He had come to Jerusalem to worship and was returning.
Acts 8:27-28

Storyline: Read Acts 8:26-40

You may have had a tremendous encounter experience. Maybe some of your retreat was wonderful and other parts lacked. It's even possible that your time away was disappointing. The first person we meet on the way back after our encounter with God is a fellow pilgrim who journeyed to Jerusalem to worship. We can imagine that this was the trip of a lifetime for this man who came all the way from Ethiopia. As a court official, it appears that he received the queen's blessing to make a trek estimated at 1500 miles (2400 km). Did he sing the Psalms of Ascents as he dreamed of his encounter with God, just as we did?

It seems as if the expectations of his time on Mount Zion may not have matched the reality of his experience. We know that foreigners would have faced restricted access to the temple. Moreover, eunuchs could not become full Jews or worship in the temple (Deuteronomy 23:1). From the text, we can glean that he came away committed but confused. He was pouring over scriptures about the Messiah but not finding answers. God honors the eunuch's faith miraculously by sending Philip to run beside him and teach him about Jesus. When we look at God's geography (and Luke's use of symbolism) in this passage, we see that even if inspiration is lacking on the mountain, God can activate his Spirit in the desert and make it a place where salvation springs up.

Maybe your encounter experience mirrors that of the eunuch. Fifteen days of spiritual preparation and all the planning it took to get away with God is a lot of effort to put into one moment. Some who put their all into these devotionals and this experience will come to today's devotional feeling a bit let down. Not only is that okay, but it's also to be expected! This story shows that God doesn't just work on top of the mountain. He can work just as powerfully on the way up and on the way back down.

We don't know everything that Philip taught the eunuch as he skillfully began teaching him from the very passage he had been reading in Isaiah. But this post-encounter reveals two sources of inspiration that the people who went to worship God on Mount Zion had limited access to: the Word of God and the Holy Spirit. In the temple era, there was only one place where God could truly be worshiped. In the church era (which Philip and the eunuch were at the very beginning of), we can worship/encounter God anywhere. We have the gospel, the scriptures (with ever-increasing accessibility), and most importantly, the Holy Spirit. Did you come down from the mountain only to find yourself in the desert? Don't fret. God will come and meet you wherever you are.

Lifeline: Chariot Ride *(Reflective Journaling)*

Like the eunuch, begin your return journey by reflecting on your encounter with God.

Briefly describe your encounter. How was the experience?

What part of your time with God was the most memorable?

Is there anything that you are disappointed about?

Is there a passage or verse that sticks in your mind? Re-read it now and write it down.

Did God "speak" to you on your retreat? Or might He be speaking to you now? How did He speak to you? What did He say?

What did you learn about God? What did you learn about yourself or others?

Is there a lasting lesson or commitment you never want to forget because of your time away?

How would you like your life to be different after having an encounter with God?

Moses' anger burned hot, and he threw the tablets out of his hands and broke them at the foot of the mountain.
Exodus 32:19

Storyline: Read Exodus 32

Moses might win the award for most dramatic return from the mountaintop. We might imagine that coming back from time away with God would be a beautiful experience. We've carved out special time, gone away, and received personal perspective from God. But the reality of our return might be more like Moses' experience than we expected.

One undeniable fact often highlighted when we spend time with God is that He is perfect, and we are not. Moreover, while we may be returning to the world with new perspective, the world itself remains the same. Our new perspective may even cause us to see the chaos of the world with more clarity. This can be discouraging or infuriating, as in the case of Moses.

Some additional perspective may help. If we look back on Moses' life, there was a time when he knew very little about God. Just as he began to wake up to the God of Israel, he murdered an Egyptian. Forty years later, God personally spoke to him through the burning bush. Moses was still quite clueless. His brother Aaron saw the power of God through the plagues and the crossing of the sea but still turned quickly to idol worship. What can we learn?

We're all on our own journey through a world full of idolatry and sin. We would do well to cherish our encounter with God without becoming more discouraged by the world. Sin and idolatry have always been reveling at the base of the mountain. We're just waking up to it by the grace of God. And surely there's still much to deal with in our own hearts that we may uncover in future encounters.

At the same time, we should take sin seriously. The law of stone that Moses smashed (and had to return up the mountain to replace) showed people just how impossible perfection is because of how holy our God is. Did God reveal sin to you during your encounter? Did a golden calf of previously unrecognized idolatry suddenly appear on your conscience? The Encounter may have revealed our hearts. The journey back down the mountain is where we deal with the things that the Spirit revealed. In this endeavor, we have an advantage over Moses because we have Jesus. Since "one greater than Moses" is here, we can confront our shortcomings with compassion and grace.

Lifeline: Seeing Sin *(Reflection and Research)*

Put sin in perspective with this journaling exercise. Get your Bible and concordance ready to research Spirit-inspired responses to sin.

Moses showed Israel their sinfulness in Exodus 32, and 3,000 were slain. Peter helped the crowd at Pentecost see their sin in Acts 2, and 3,000 were saved. Jesus changes the way we see sin. It's not because sin is less serious or because the God of the Old Testament is less gracious than the God of the New Testament. They are the same God. The difference is that sin has been dealt with once and for all.

Did God reveal a personal sin or idol during your encounter? (All sin is a type of idol worship.) If so, what?

Can you think of any New Testament passages that reveal how Jesus would have you deal with your sin?

Did God reveal someone else's sin or idolatry while you were on retreat? If so, what?

Can you think of any passages that reveal how Jesus would want you to help someone else overcome sin?

Did you see the sins of our society more clearly while you were away with God? How?

Write down any passages that can give perspective on the sinfulness of our society and God's perfect plan for our world.

And he said, "Who are you Lord?"
Acts 9:5

Storyline: Read Acts 9:1-19

Saul's encounter with God changed him and changed the whole world. In the aftermath of meeting God on the road to Damascus, God transformed the church's greatest persecutor into the church's greatest champion. Before his fateful trip to Damascus, Saul was quite confident in his knowledge of who God was. He was so sure of his view of God that he oversaw the execution of Stephen and was on the hunt for other Christ followers. Yet, when he actually heard the voice of God, his response tells us that he had no idea who God was. The flashing light that blinded him also opened his eyes to how blind he had been the whole time.

Encounters with God have a way of shaking up our foundations. As we go about our regular routines, we have ideas about God (theology) that shape us, often without knowing. We don't regularly stop and reflect on what we think about God. But when we have a memorable encounter with God, he can reveal himself to us more fully. We might imagine that seeing God in a new way is exciting. But it can also be uncomfortable. Our hearts may even resist accepting new ideas about God. Did God speak to you during your retreat? Did he reveal new (to you) aspects of his character? Did you feel excited or shaken up when you saw God in a new light?

In scripture, visions of God often happen in pairs. There are a couple of reasons for this: 1) When we are the only person who sees something about God, we are likely in error. The testimony of another witness can give us good reason to be confident about what God is showing us. 2) When our foundations are shaken, we need the encouragement of others who are also seeing God.

As Saul had his vision on the road to Damascus, a Godly disciple named Ananias received a complimentary vision inside the city. The message that Ananias heard from Jesus was also hard to accept. He was commanded to risk his life to minister to a murderer. Interestingly, it was only after Ananias met with Saul that the scales fell from his eyes so he could see again. He immediately got baptized, and the rest is history. A history that any person of non-Jewish lineage can look back on and praise God, Saul, and Ananias for.

Lifeline: Finding your Ananias *(Fellowship)*

As you attempt to process your encounter, you may need the help of a fellow disciple to gain clarity on the next steps God may be planning for your life.

In what ways might you be walking around with scales on your eyes? Do you feel like you should have had some great revelation during your time away with God? God's revelation may be waiting for you in a conversation with a trusted brother or sister.

Take a moment to pray about the people God has placed in your life. Ask God who he'd like you to share your encounter experience with. Call or text that person and schedule a time to discuss your retreat. The rest of this page can be completed during or after you meet with your Ananias.

Post-Meeting Reflections:
How was the experience of relating your encounter with God?

What perspective did you gain from this conversation?

What did God reveal to you about himself because of your time of focused fellowship?

What did God teach you about the friend that you met up with?

It's easy to take fellowship for granted. How does this experience deepen your appreciation for fellowship?

Bring God into the conversation by praying for your Ananias.

**If your friend also participated in the Encounter, write down the activities they chose in the Menu of the Encounter section.

After three days they found him in the temple.
Luke 2:46

Storyline: Read Luke 2:41-52

Sometimes the best way to find yourself is to get lost. Jesus' trip to Mount Zion as a preteen lasted a few days longer than planned. Like you, he would have traveled with fellow worshipers singing the Psalms of Ascents up to an encounter with God. And possibly, like you, after the official time with God was over, he was a little lost. For us, and for him, lostness is a matter of perspective. Jesus' parents were understandably distraught by their error. Jesus, however, seemed completely unflustered. In fact, while others perceived him as lost, he felt quite at home.

It's possible that your encounter with God has left you feeling a little lost. If Jesus was left behind after spending special time with God, then there's a good chance the same thing could happen to us. Have you felt more uncertain about your faith after your encounter? Have things been less clear? Are you seeking direction but not finding clarity? Things may begin to make sense if you accept that lostness is not necessarily negative. Jesus filled his time of lostness up by "sitting among the teachers, listening to them and asking them questions." After his extended encounter, he "went down with [his parents] and came to Nazareth and was submissive to them." It sounds like he came out of lostness with a very clear vision.

This booklet has focused on the experience of God's people on the mountaintop. But God speaks to his people in all sorts of "geographies." In scripture, the sea, the garden, the valley, the desert/wilderness, and more, are all places where God encounters his people. Lostness is often associated with the wilderness. We can look to the clear example of Israel in Exodus to see that a few days on the mountain won't automatically take you out of the wilderness. In fact, the encounter on the mountain sometimes reveals that we've got some wandering ahead of us, just like it did for Israel at Sinai.

But the mountaintop experience reveals something else: The geography we find ourselves in when we return from our encounter doesn't matter as much as the fact that God's presence is waiting for us in each landscape. Imagine the fear and uncertainty that Mary and Joseph must have felt as they frantically searched Jerusalem. After three days, they not only found their son but also God, present in his temple, in the person of Jesus Christ. Likewise, our lostness is never permanent. Later in Luke, after another three-day wait, the presence of God in each of our lives was revealed and secured by the resurrection.

Lifeline: A Humble Disposition in God's Presence *(Posture)*

For the next ten days, our lifelines will follow a new direction. Dr. David Pocta's research on spiritual wilderness has revealed ten postures that can help us navigate our faith journey even when we are no longer on the mountaintop with God. Each day we'll examine practical ways to live in these postures as we seek the presence of God in our day-to-day life.

During the last supper, in the Gospel of John, Jesus tells his disciples that it was necessary for him to go away so that God's presence through the Holy Spirit could come. Jesus comforts his disciples before his death by saying, "It is to your advantage that I go away, for if I do not, the Helper will not come to you." (John 16:7) Thus, the amazing reality for the Christian is that we live in the constant presence of God. Where Jesus' parents (and all who came before him) had to go to the temple to find the presence of God, we are the temple that God now dwells in. Yet, how often do we recognize the presence of God through his Spirit in our lives? How many of us are like renters who don't realize that they have a (very special) roommate? Are we going about our lives as if we are alone when the reality is we always have the most extraordinary presence with us? How can we be humble to God's presence and leading in our lives if we can't even remember He is present?

An Exercise:

The New Testament word for spirit and breath (pneuma) are the same. Even in English, inspiration and respiration share the same root. Today we're going to use our breath to remember the presence of the Spirit in our lives today. After all, Jesus breathed his Spirit into his disciples later in John. (20:22) When we start to get upset, we are often told to take a deep breath, which usually helps us reflect and reset. Let's use our breath to reflect on the fact that Jesus is present with us and reset our hearts to the reality that we have a spiritual roommate. Here's how:

Set the alarm on your phone or watch to vibrate at the top of every hour (or at convenient intervals). When the alarm goes off, simply take one deep breath, and think about the presence of Jesus.

Try to do this during your waking hours until tomorrow's devotional. Before you begin tomorrow's devotional, answer the following questions:

How did breathing and reflecting on the presence of the Spirit change your day? Did you feel more humble and reliant on God? How could you continue to practice the presence of God?

In your offspring shall all the nations of the earth be blessed, because you have obeyed my voice.
Genesis 22:18

Storyline: Read Genesis 22

Abraham's ascent up the mountain, encounter with God, and descent is legendary. The innocent and awkward question from Isaac serves to heighten the drama as he unknowingly carries the wood for his own sacrificial pyre. At first glance, we might read this narrative and wonder if God is being cruel. After all, Abraham has already proven faithful multiple times before this. Our adverse reaction may stem from a misunderstanding of what it means to be tested by God. When a company gets to the testing phase, the product has already gone through much growth to get to a place where it can be thoroughly tested before it is ready for market. The only products that get tested are the ones that are thoroughly believed in. If a company doesn't believe in its product, they won't bother testing it. This is how and why God tests us. He wasn't trying to make Abraham stumble. Instead, He believed that Abraham could be even more faithful than he had already been. He wanted to show the world the heights of the patriarch's trust in God. Abraham passes the test! Have you felt tested by God? If you adopt this perspective, how do the tests you are facing reveal God's faith in you? In what way might he believe you are strong enough to display his glory?

The result of Abraham's faithful obedience was the greatest promise yet. If we track the promises that God makes to Abraham beginning in Genesis 12, they just get better and better. This last one in 22:18 seems impossible. How can all nations be blessed by one man's offspring? One man's offspring is only one nation. We know that Jesus makes this promise possible as all who believe in him are children of the promise. (See Galatians 3)

As impossible as this test seems to us, not to mention Abraham, the blessing for obedience is even more astounding. We get hints of the enormity of the blessing in this passage. The mountain is called Moriah. This means something like "God will see it through" or "The Lord will provide." Here, God provided the first substitutive sacrifice, trading Isaac for a ram. But this was not the last. Mount Moriah is the same as Mount Zion. This is the mount that the temple and its sacrificial system would be built upon. This is the mountain that Jesus would be led across after his arrest to face trial and be sentenced to death. Unlike Abraham, God did not stop his own son from being sacrificed with a substitution. Instead, Jesus passed the ultimate test and became the substitution for our sin. On the mountain of the Lord, God did indeed provide and see it through.

Lifeline: Listen to the Divine Voice *(Posture)*

"Listening" has two meanings that are both important. We must be able to hear in the first place. Then we have to act upon what we hear if we are to truly listen.

Abraham listened to God in both senses of the word. He was tuned in to God. When God spoke, he was ready, saying, "Here I am."

What did you hear from God on your personal retreat? How did God speak to you? What did he say?

That may be a strange question or a stretch for us. Many have been taught that God only speaks through the Bible. Yet, when we read our Bibles, God speaks in many ways! When He speaks to us outside of scripture, He will never contradict the Word. But that doesn't mean He can't speak to us through silence, meditation, our consciences, or other Godly people.

What has God been saying to you in the days after your retreat? What's been sticking in your mind or heart?

Now that you've taken a moment to listen to the Divine Voice consider if you've also listened by being obedient to what you've heard.

How can you begin to practice what God has been telling you?

God's words to Abraham must have been so hard to hear. We often talk about having faith in God but fail to consider how much faith He has in us.

What are you hearing from the Divine Voice that is difficult?

What promise or blessing might be waiting on the other side of truly listening to God?

I have uttered what I did not understand,
Things too wonderful for me, which I did not know...
I had heard of you by the hearing of the ear,
But now my eyes see you.
Job 42:3-5

Storyline: Read Job 42

Satan tempts us, hoping that we will fail. But, as we saw in yesterday's devotional, God tests us, believing we will succeed. In the moment, it can be very difficult to know the difference. The struggle of being tempted and tested is painfully illustrated in the life of Job. His ascent to an encounter with God is devastating to his family and his health. His well-meaning but misguided friends swoop in but provide no comfort. His saga culminates in one of the most epic encounters in all of scripture. God speaks to him out of a whirlwind, repeating the refrain, "Were you there?" Job is humbled to his core as God interrogates him regarding the creation and function of the world. It all hammers home the big idea that there will be many things in this life and with God that we will never understand.

In the aftermath of his encounter with God, Job is doubly blessed. God honors his words and restores his family and health. Interestingly, much of what Job expressed during his suffering sounds like doubt. He says things like:
"Why do you hide your face and count me your enemy?"
"You destroy the hope of man."
"The graveyard is ready for me."
"I call for help but there is no justice."

We might think that if we spoke to God like Job, we would be punished. Yet, Job is praised for faithfulness, even though his words often sound quite faithless. What's going on? Just like so many of the faithful heroes of scripture, Job struggled with faith. They openly doubted God. If we were to come to Job as he scratched at his open sores, we might agree with his friends that he was a lost cause. It would seem as if God's judgment on Job was clear. But there's a paradox and tension that must be maintained if we are to have true faith: doubt is a part of faith.

If we don't feel the freedom to question God (he's big enough to handle our doubts), then are we freely following God or just keeping in line with a religion? It's okay to doubt and express those doubts. On a practical note, when we share our faith struggles with others, it is important to express them to better friends than Job's. Look for counselors who will help you be more faithful on the other side of whatever test God has set before you.

Lifeline: The Courage to Doubt *(Posture)*

Job teaches us how to doubt faithfully. Although it may seem like an oxymoron, it's essential if we're going to stay faithful for the long haul.

Dealing with Doubt:
Almost every faithful person has doubts from time to time. We can feel guilty for doubting and try to suppress our doubts, or we can deal with our doubt. We deal with doubt by allowing ourselves to be honest with our thoughts and feelings and then expressing those thoughts (the good, the bad, and the ugly) to God and to faithful friends. Our doubts may take many forms. We may even doubt His existence altogether, but more likely, we'll occasionally doubt things like His promises, presence, or grace.

Think back on your encounter with God and the time before and afterward. It may be very difficult to admit, but it is so important if you seek a real relationship with God. What are your doubts? In what ways is it hard to trust God?

Now that you've named your doubts, it's essential to deal with them in a healthy way.

Start by talking to God. Tell God about your doubts in prayer. After you pray, take a moment to write down how you feel or any insight you gained:

Next, identify a few people you could be real with and receive encouragement (not condemnation) and help from. When we admit our struggles, many people may try and come to our aid. It's human nature to show empathy and want to help. It's essential that we get help from sources that will lead us to God and not away from God. Just because friends, co-workers, teachers, and counselors are well-meaning, it doesn't mean they will be helpful.

Write down the names of your potential helpers and say a prayer for them to be guided by the Spirit:

In the end, it takes so much courage to admit that we doubt God sometimes. Like Job, may our honest doubts lead us to double blessing.

But Mary treasured up all these things, pondering them in her heart.
Luke 2:19

Storyline: Luke 2, John 19:17-27

Mary, the mother of Jesus, is a striking figure in the gospels and Christian faith traditions for a good reason. When presented with a near-impossible task, she displays trust and maturity beyond her years. As she raises the most special child the world has ever known, she postures herself with a confounding openness and humility.

Ronald Rolheiser, in his book, "Sacred Fire," contrasts Mary's pondering heart with the amazement of the crowds that Jesus interacted with. Amazement or astonishment is the go-to response of the masses. Jesus is not impressed by amazement. As Rolheiser describes it, amazement is simply a conduit that passes an idea along without reflecting or filtering it through a lens of faith or gospel. It's a mindless spreading of emotion or information. Jesus often responded negatively to amazement, saying things like, "Why are you amazed?"

Pondering, on the other hand, as illustrated by Mary, takes information in, reflects with an open heart toward God, and then releases it back into the world redeemed, spiritualized, or filtered by the gospel. As viral videos and social media memes rule society's conversations, people who ponder instead of passing on are exceptional. We have more access to amazing and astonishing things than ever before. Are we content with simply passing on worldly ideas? Or, like Mary, will we take the time to process what is happening with a humble, open, and Spirit-led heart? When we ponder like Mary, we are a levy for the viral nature of the world and a filter that injects God into the mundane.

John gives us an incredibly powerful image of Mary pondering. She is there at the foot of the cross. And that's all we know. She is not crying out. She is not raging against injustice. She is simply standing there. She is pondering, even as her son dies. In this, Mary teaches us one last lesson about the power of pondering. When we act as filters and not just conduits, we can take what the world is dishing out and redeem it. But sometimes, the things the world offers should not be passed on, even if filtered through a gospel mindset. In those moments, one who ponders like Mary can display the greatest possible fortitude by witnessing wickedness but not returning it in kind or passing it on. When we ponder, our desire for justice can be shelved so that evil will spread no further. We can just take it in and be content that it won't be passed on. Such is the power of pondering.

Lifeline: The Fortitude to Ask Tough Questions *(Posture)*

Patient pondering seems to be a lost art in our world. Religion often teaches or at least implies that asking questions is not what faithful people do. True faith can ponder the most difficult questions, process them, and send them out into the world redeemed. Let's work on the posture of pondering:

Strong Enough to Be Weak

Like the doubts we dealt with yesterday, we often view questions that we have about God negatively. But real faith asks real questions without fear. Jesus came for the sick, not the healthy. When we pretend we don't have questions or already know all the answers, we pretend to be healthy and without need. In reality, we all have significant needs – and God has the answer to all our needs. Are you strong enough to admit weakness? Do you know enough to realize what you don't know?

Take a moment to ponder some of the big questions you have. Maybe these are things you've been afraid to think about. Maybe there are places that you've tried to keep your heart from going. Go ahead and ask the tough questions. Write them down in the space below.

Now that you've pondered and journaled some tough questions put your questions before God in prayer. There's no question He can't handle.

How does it feel to be honest with God?

Even after talking to God, many of your questions may remain unanswered. There is so much we will not know this side of eternity, but having the fortitude to ask tough questions means that even if we don't know the answers to our questions, we'll get to know God more just because we had the courage to ask and be real – and that answers our greatest need.

Then Jesus was led up by the Spirit into the wilderness to be tempted by the devil.
Matthew 4:1

Storyline: Matthew 3:13-4:17

Have you ever wondered what it would be like to read the Bible for the first time with no prior knowledge about what happens? We would probably be shocked by so many of the things that we've become familiar with. What happens after Jesus' encounter with God at his baptism would certainly surprise us. Even the sentence highlighted at the top of this page doesn't end like we would expect if we didn't already know the story. "Jesus was led up by the Spirit." Surely what follows will be good. To what heights will the Spirit lead Jesus? But then, as the sentence continues, we learn that the Spirit is leading Jesus into the wilderness or desert. That's a place of confusion and struggle throughout scripture. Why would the Spirit lead Jesus there? But it gets worse! As the verse comes to an end, we see that the Spirit is leading Jesus into the wilderness so that he can be tempted by the devil. Why would the Holy Spirit lead Jesus in that way? What is happening?

Let's ask ourselves the same question. What has been happening since you had your encounter? Where has the Spirit led you? If it's been challenging, you're in good company. Jesus had an encounter with the Father before he started his ministry. The heavens broke open, and God spoke words of supreme encouragement. The Spirit descended upon him like a dove. Talk about an incredible encounter with God! But this was immediately followed by the Spirit leading Jesus into the sparseness of the desert and a challenging encounter with the accuser himself.

Many Christians don't think about the Spirit enough. When we do, we probably think of Him as more of an encouraging presence or emotional support. Matthew does not try to soften his explanation of the Spirit's work after Jesus' baptism. Jesus describes the Spirit in John 3 to Nicodemus as a wind that blows wherever it pleases. Contrary to our expectation of peace, a Spirit-led life is often windblown. In fact, one of the functions of the Spirit is to lead us into the testing that we've learned about in recent devotionals. Internalizing this truth can reframe the seemingly random trials we face in life. This may not be our favorite characteristic of the Spirit, but this nudging is essential. What if Jesus hadn't gone into the wilderness and experienced victory over the tempter? What if Peter hadn't taken that bold step out of the boat? What if the Spirit hadn't led you into a past challenge and helped you overcome? We can read about trusting God through hard times. But true clarity and confidence come from experience. Thank you, Holy Spirit, for leading us to places we would never lead ourselves.

Lifeline: Willingness to be Led by the Spirit into Uncharted Waters *(Posture)*

Uncharted waters, barren wilderness, bustling cities; the Spirit works everywhere. The question is not, is the Spirit working? But rather, are you willing to be led into the Spirit's work?

Seeing the Spirit

One of the reasons we might have a hard time connecting with the Holy Spirit is not because He is invisible but because we are looking in the wrong places. There's a saying, "Give credit where credit is due." Many of the things we credit to chance or even to Satan may actually be the work of the Holy Spirit. Consider how the Spirit bookends the saga of Israel in the Old Testament. He leads His people in the Promised Land through a pillar of cloud and fire for 40 years in the wilderness while an entire generation dies. And then, after a few centuries in the land, He leads them into exile. The closing chapters of 2 Kings, 2 Chronicles, and Jeremiah reflect the struggle that God's people had at that time to see God's Spirit as the initiator of something so devastating. How difficult it must have been to see the Spirit's leadership in those times. There's a part of us that doesn't want to credit God with anything negative. But his perspective is so much larger. The negatives we see can be a part of the Spirit's work for our benefit and for blessing in the world.

In Matthew 8, immediately after another mountaintop experience (the sermon on the mount), Jesus is approached by a man with leprosy. Jesus is often the one asking the questions in the gospels, but here, the infected man leads with an interesting question. "Lord, if you are willing..." He calls Jesus Lord. He knows that Jesus has the power to heal. But, as an untouchable in society, with an incurable and contagious disease, he was unsure if Jesus had the openness and desire (the will) to heal him. Jesus answers immediately, "I am willing." And he took an extra step to demonstrate how willing he was. He reaches out and touches the leprous man. Jesus certainly could have healed him with just a word, as he demonstrated on multiple occasions. But, in touching the man, he shows what it means to be willing. It's a stretch, a reach.

It may seem like a strange parallel, but the Holy Spirit is like this man with leprosy. He is mostly invisible to society. He doesn't demand action but asks politely. He needs us to take action to help heal this world or at least help it not get sicker. Yes, the Holy Spirit is asking, "Are you willing?" Like Jesus being led into the desert, like Israel being led into exile, the way that the Spirit leads the willing is often dangerous. Touching a man with leprosy! We romanticize adventure until we actually find ourselves in the middle of one. Then we groan for relief. What adventure does the Spirit have waiting for you? How will the wind blow through your life? You'll only find out if you're willing.

Pray a prayer of willingness. Stretch out your hand as you offer yourself to God.

And Jacob was left alone. And a man wrestled with him until the breaking of the day.
Genesis 32:24

Storyline: Genesis 32:22-32

What a wild night! Jacob is already under a great deal of stress as he fears reuniting with his older brother Esau. Fearing retribution for stealing his birthright and blessing, he sends his family and possessions across the river, where they will be safer. He is left alone.

Or so he thinks. A man appears out of nowhere and wrestles with him all night long. Jacob is injured but refuses to give up. As day breaks, he begs for the man's name. After wrestling all night, he's beginning to realize that this may be more than a man. At the end of the encounter, he names the place Peniel, which means "Face of God."

In summary, Jacob believes he is wrestling in the night with a person, but his struggle reveals to him that he's actually wrestling with God. He comes away limping but blessed.

What have you been struggling with in the darkness? Who have you been wrestling with? What if you tried to see the face of God in your struggle?

Like doubting and questioning, we often view wrestling negatively. When we are wrestling through hardships or struggling with people, we can be slow to see God's role. God is a wrestler. He changes Jacob's name to Israel, which means "Wrestles with God." God's people are defined by the struggle they will have with their God. It can be so difficult for us to shake the idea that after we're baptized, everything will get easier. The truth is, we are baptized into generations of God strugglers who persevered, got blessed, and probably came out limping. Wrestling through the darkness is a faithful and necessary activity. It is God-initiated, even if it takes us a while to see that the problems and people we think we are wrestling with have often been divinely appointed so that we can grow in our faith.

Lifeline: The audacity to wrestle with God and personal faith *(Posture)*

What or who have you been wrestling with? Bold faith means facing our struggles by looking for the face of God in the darkness.

Face to Face
We often carry our struggles without realizing the weight of our burdens. Leaving life behind and being alone with God like Jacob can bring our struggles to light. Maybe while you were on your personal retreat, a struggle seemed to come out of nowhere. It is normal and good for God's people to wrestle.

What have you been wrestling with? Was there something that kept coming into your mind during the quiet moments of your encounter? Is there a faith issue that has you limping into your devotional times or church meetings?

Go ahead and write down anything that comes to mind:

New Moves
High School wrestlers will tell you that learning new moves is essential. If you only use the same basic moves, you'll end up on your back. New moves are an opportunity to grow and to win more often.

What we often want, and even pray for, is for our struggles to end. We want to be done wrestling. But God is a wrestler. In many ways, to quit wrestling is to quit God. Instead of giving up or giving in, we can seek God's face in our struggle with new moves. The recipes you tried during the encounter were new moves.

What would happen if you applied your new moves to your struggle? New moves can only be learned through repetition.

A few of the Encounter recipes can be especially helpful when we find ourselves wrestling in life and with God. **Apply one of these new moves to your struggle by looking back at the Encounter section:**

Prayer of Examen: Talk to God about your day every night with this prayer template.

Face to Face: Have you set up your tent of meeting?

A Three-fold Cord: Many of our struggles are relational. Have you brought God into your relational wrestling matches?

And when they saw him they worshiped him, but some doubted.

Matthew 28:17

Storyline: Matthew 28:16-20

This is a familiar passage, and for a good reason. Just before his ascension to heaven, Jesus' final words in Matthew are known as the Great Commission. His command to "Go and make disciples of all nations" has been a rallying cry for disciples through the ages. When this passage is shared from the pulpit, preachers often begin in verse 18, skipping the context the two preceding verses provide. O, what encouragement we miss when we preach the Great Commission while ignoring the great commotion that the disciples were dealing with!

This passage begins by reminding us that there are only 11 disciples. Jesus himself couldn't keep everyone faithful. We put so much pressure on ourselves in regard to the mission. We think we are supposed to save souls and help them persevere. We feel like failures when people don't come to God or when they leave.

The eleven meet the risen Jesus at a pre-determined mountain in Galilee. Tradition tells us that this could be Mount Arbel. From Arbel, the weary disciples could look out and see the Mount of Beatitudes, where Jesus gave the new law. (Matthew 5-7) They could see the Sea of Galilee and remember the calming of the storm and walking on the waves. Here on this mountain, Jesus stood before them, having been crucified and buried, and yet undeniably, he was alive.

What Matthew tells us next about the disciples is shocking: "They worshiped him, but some doubted." How, in this moment, in this place, with Jesus before them, could they have any doubts at all? Matthew's honesty is striking. It should bolster our faith in the Bible that Matthew would be so real. At the very last moment, some of Jesus' closest disciples still struggled to believe. Would you include that in your gospel? More likely, it would end, "And everyone believed, and you should too."

In our descent, we've been dealing with issues that may have bubbled to the surface during our time away. Questions, doubts, struggles. The context before the Great Commission may be just as important as the commission itself. Even the best disciples must worship through their doubts sometimes. And those worshiping doubters are the exact people to whom Jesus entrusts his saving mission. He didn't shrug his shoulders and find newer, more faithful disciples. He trusted these doubters just like he trusts us.

Lifeline: The faith to believe in the living word of God *(Posture)*

Despite their doubts, the eleven disciples went on to change the world by obediently following Jesus' command. What will God accomplish through you if you obey through the doubts?

Hard To Believe
There are a couple of ways that something can be hard to believe. 1) A story can be so wild that we literally have a hard time believing it. 2) Something can be hard to believe because we know that if we believe it, it will change our whole lives.

The gospel is hard to believe in both ways. If you're reading this, then you probably have the first kind of unbelief figured out most of the time. But the second kind of unbelief may be harder to overcome. Interestingly, Jesus does not directly address the doubts that his disciples are feeling. Instead, he begins his last command with a statement of authority, a statement of truth about reality. In our increasingly relativistic society, we can forget that there is one truth, not many truths. Jesus drops truth: All authority has been given to him. You can believe it or not, but it doesn't change the reality.

Beyond Belief
We typically wait to act or obey until we believe. Faith should come first. That sounds Christian, right? Maybe not. Facts are more important than faith. Picture your spirituality like a train with three cars. The engine in the front represents Fact (truth). Facts are what we want to move us down the track. The coal car in the middle is Faith. Our faith fires us up and should fuel the engine of truth. Last is the caboose, which houses our Feelings. Feelings are important. They are a part of the train, and they need to go down the track with us. But when we put our faith in our feelings instead of facts, we go nowhere but backward.

Often, the real struggle isn't whether we believe. It's if we're willing to do what the word of God commands even when our faith is low, or there's not much fuel in the coal car. The eleven went and made disciples of all nations, baptized them, and taught them to obey everything, even though their faith wasn't 100%. (And as disciples 2,000 years later, we should be so grateful.)

Who may be waiting for you to obey even when you don't feel like it? What part of your life can you begin to change even before your heart is totally in it?

Jesus concludes with the greatest promise of all. He will be with us. He's not just on the mountain. He's with us every step of the way. Whether we believe it or not.

It's been a week since your encounter. Pray to feel God's presence and know that his promise is enough.

I brought him to your disciples, and they could not heal him.
Matthew 17:16

Storyline: Mark 9:2-29

From the highest heights to immediate chaos. Jesus' encounter with the Father, Moses, and Elijah on the Mount of Transfiguration is one of the great moments in all of scripture. Yet even Jesus has to descend from the mountain. And what does he descend to? He finds his disciples quarreling with an angry crowd and failing to be effective ministers.

The father of a demon-possessed boy yells above the crowd and gets Jesus up to speed. The disciples had been asked to cast out the demon but were unable. Jesus responds to the news by mourning the faithlessness of the people and asking for the child to be brought before him. A conversation ensues. Jesus (who already knows all things) asks the father an empathetic question to reveal his heart. "How long has this been happening to him?" The boy's father wonders if Jesus can do anything to help. Jesus is taken aback. As readers, we might be tempted to shake our heads at the man's lack of faith. Matthew just had us on the Mount of Transfiguration. Where is this guy's faith?

I wonder, though, if we had transcripts of our prayers, how many times would we find the phrase "if you can?" The boy's father responds, "I believe, help my unbelief!" That sentence barely makes sense, and yet there may be no better way to describe our faith on most days. If we're honest, at our best, we believe, and we need help from Jesus to overcome our unbelief at the same time.

After the demon is driven out and Jesus is again alone with his disciples, they ask him why they were unable to drive out the demon. Jesus tells them, "This kind cannot be driven out by anything but prayer." Interestingly, Mark does not record a prayer from Jesus in this passage. But there is a prayer. Jesus' conversation with the boy's father causes him to pray unknowingly to Jesus. He cries out to the Lord, "I believe, help me overcome my unbelief." And it is after that accidental and honest prayer that the demon can finally be exorcised.

This is why we have to keep encountering God and not just go through the motions of devotional times. Here, the encounter, the conversation, the listening, and the honesty all work together to bring healing. The disciples went through the motions of how to cast out a demon without effect. An encounter with Jesus allowed a man who wasn't even a disciple of Jesus to pray the prayer that released his son from bondage. How can you build more encounters into your life?

Lifeline: The mettle to overcome limiting dogma *(Posture)*

Regardless of our faith tradition, we have traditions and theologies that both help and hinder our connection to God and our impact in the world.

"Why could we not cast it out?"
The nine disciples who were not invited up to the Mount of Transfiguration stayed busy. Like Moses, when he ascended Sinai to receive the law, a crowd gathered at the base of the mountain. Jesus did not return to a golden calf, but that doesn't mean there wasn't idol worship to deal with at the base of the mountain. Could the demon represent the idol of religiosity?

Look at how the demon affects the boy. "He grinds his teeth and becomes rigid.' These are the same words that Jesus uses to describe the Pharisees. Jesus asks the father how long it's been like this, and he responds, "From childhood."

Since the founding of our faith, we've been in a battle against religiosity. The temptation and trajectory of movements in Christianity tends toward rigid pride, gnashing teeth, and ultimately, destruction. We start with childlike faith, open to new experiences, and seeing the scriptures with wide eyes and soft hearts. But even in spiritual infancy, the demon of dogma can affect churches and individuals. And once possessed, this demon can be tough to drive out.

The boy's father shows us the way. He's been disappointed. The group of Christians he went to for help said the right things but didn't actually help. They just ended up a quarreling crowd as so often happens in churches. He separates himself from the crowd and personally initiates with Jesus. He is open. He is honest. He deals with his faith history. He prays with desperation and passion. The demon is removed!

Are you struggling under the oppression of the demon of dogma? As you've "matured" spiritually, have you become overly religious? Has the wide-open heart that led to your conversion become a narrow mind? Right doctrine is essential, but the desire for right doctrine can cause us to become rigid.

How can we know if we're too focused on being right and missing out on true righteousness? Jesus says, "You will recognize them by their fruits." (Matthew 7:16) What good is being "right" if our rigidity is causing us to miss out on the miraculous? This can be so difficult! After losing his demon, the boy looks dead. But Jesus lifts him up to new life.

Ask God to show you any areas in your life where you may have begun to bow to the demon of dogma. Ask him for the strength and the faith to have a soft heart that breaks through self-imposed limits and is willing to believe even in unbelief.

So he departed from there and found Elisha.
1 Kings 19:19

Storyline: 1 Kings 19

In your encounter on the mountain, you focused on friendship with God. We need God to meet us where we are and to be our friend. But we need people too. This is exactly how God ministers to Elijah after a pair of epic encounters. Elijah's first encounter, on Mount Carmel, involved calling fire from heaven and seeing hundreds of false prophets slain. He followed this up by making it rain (literally). Unfortunately, his descent down the mountain also seemed to be a descent into despair. We should not ignore this. Sometimes, after intense moments with God, our emotions and our minds can be overwhelmed. Elijah just wanted to lie down and die. Have you ever been that exhausted?

God meets Elijah where he's at and strengthens him so he can have another encounter. This time, on Mount Sinai, God reveals himself to the prophet in a low whisper. At the end of the conversation, God gives Elijah a command that seems to come from nowhere. He's struggling with his faith, his confidence, and what seems like depression. Even an encounter with God isn't enough to lift him from his fog. God offers this solution: Go find three people from three very different backgrounds.

The first two on the list are kings. Hazael is to be anointed king over Syria, and Jehu will be king over Israel. Hazael will eventually begin to destroy Israel. That certainly classifies as different backgrounds. The third person on the list is Elisha. Elisha is the most dissimilar. He is just a farmer. But Elijah calls him to be his attendant and to take over the mantle of prophet.

Interestingly, if we read the rest of Elijah's story, we see that he only anoints Elisha and doesn't get to the kings. He goes to Elisha first and calls him to consider what it will mean to follow in his footsteps, much like how Jesus called his disciples. Elisha accepts. Before Elijah gets a chance to anoint the kings that God prescribed, he is taken up in a whirlwind, and Elisha is given a double portion of Elijah's spirit. Elisha goes on to finish the job that Elijah was given. Elijah anointed one person. Elisha anoints two kings with his double-portioned spirit.

Have you ever wondered why and how Elijah ended up only doing one-third of what God asked? What if, like most of the things God asks of us, the task was really for Elijah more than it was for God? Elijah needed a friend. And God saw to it that Elijah wouldn't die alone in the wilderness. But instead, his new friend would walk with him until the end.

Lifeline: The need for a widened community *(Posture)*

Just as our traditions and theologies can become too narrow, our relationships can become myopic, especially as we get older. How could a widened community bear fruit in your life?

"Then he arose and went after Elijah."
Let's think about 1 Kings 19:19-21 from Elisha's perspective. He's just out in the field riding on a plow behind a pair of oxen, and a stranger comes out of the woods and puts his cloak around him. Prophets wore distinct garments in this time, so Elisha would have immediately known what he was being called to. Elijah allows him to say goodbye to his family but urges him to think about what it means to wear the prophet's mantle and follow him. Elisha shows that he understood the gravity of the situation by burning his plowing equipment and cooking his oxen for an epic last meal with his family. There would be no going back. Elisha was committed to his relationship with Elijah.

There have been many studies that confirm what we likely already know as we get older. The older we get, the less relationships we have. And the relationships that we do have are more likely to be people who are a lot like us. Maybe it's because we end up living near people in the same socioeconomic class, or perhaps it's because we just get grouchy as we age. Whatever the reason, if we end up with fewer friendships and less diverse friendships (in all the ways), we're missing out!

One of the practical things we can glean from Elijah and Elisha is that deep relationships take commitment and work. When we were young, we could just ask someone on the playground if they would play with us. New friendships were easy to come by. We are told that Elisha "went after Elijah." He had to pursue this new apprenticeship and friendship. It must have taken work to learn about a new person and a new calling. Are you willing to put in the work and go after new and diverse relationships?

Surely, the learning curve from farmer to miracle-working prophet was steep. Likewise, we have so much to learn from new and diverse relationships. What could you learn from someone ten years older or younger than you? How would your relationship with God be impacted by a friend who is part of a different faith community? How would your life be enriched by deeper friendships with people from different backgrounds than yours?

Wondering where to start? Think back to the playground. Friendships are easy when we do things together. Is there a hobby, club, or activity that you've been wanting to try? Take your post-encounter self into new territory and go after new relationships.

Our God whom we serve is able to deliver us from the burning fiery furnace.
Daniel 3:17

Storyline: Daniel 3

Daniel's friends have a different kind of encounter. Instead of a special time of worship with the true God, they are ushered into a time of forced idol worship. They are expected to bow to a false image while a Babylonian worship band plays in the background. The crowd obeys, prostrating themselves before the ultimate icon of worldly success, a golden statue of Nebuchadnezzar. Except three men stay on their feet. Can you imagine how Shadrach, Meshach, and Abednego must have stood out among the crowd?

We are not the only people having worship experiences. Empires and idols still demand that the crowds bow low before them. Your experience with God away from the world ministered to your soul, but it may have also served to alienate you from people who don't see God the way you do.

Have you shared your experience with co-workers, neighbors, or friends? When we get excited about a new diet or exercise routine, we can't help but share about it. We almost automatically share about things that work. If your encounter worked on your heart, you should certainly share it. If you are excited about what God is doing in your life or about what's happening in your church, tell someone.

But know this: You might be entering into the fire. And that's okay. When we share our faith with expectations that we will be well-received, we are setting ourselves up for disappointment. There is no biblical promise that people will respond favorably to our evangelism, invitations, or conversations about faith. In fact, the opposite is true. Sharing often leads to suffering. Jesus even promises persecution. (John 15:20)

All of this might cause us to think twice before standing out among the crowds and sharing about Jesus. But if we can internalize this truth, we'll actually share our faith with more frequency and joy. Yes, we are promised persecution. But we are also promised presence. Just as a fourth figure appeared in the fire, Jesus promises that when we "go and make disciples," he will "be with us always." We are not guaranteed success. Take the pressure off. Don't share because it's something you are required to do. Is Jesus working in your life? We love to share about things that work. Show your friends the difference Jesus is making, and let God do the rest.

Lifeline: The faith to accept the journey's outcome *(Posture)*

Our final posture puts us in a position of surrender before God.

"Our God is able to deliver us...but if not"
These three words, by these three exiles, might be the most faithful words in all of scripture. "But if not." Was this spoken as they began to smell the smoke from the furnace as it was heated up? Nebuchadnezzar is the most powerful person on the planet. They show no signs of intimidation or anxiety. They did something special for God and trusted him with the outcome.

Maybe you haven't realized it, but you've also made a special stand for your faith. Spending quality time in the word of God and going on retreat pits you against the world. Working on your heart, character, and spirituality is commendable. Indeed, this journey up to encounter and back down is a lot of things, but one thing it's not is in your control. We can put in the work, but we can't decide the outcome. This is true of a 30-day focus or a 30-year walk with God. Our world makes this reality difficult to accept. We are used to pushing a button and getting exactly what we want. With God, sometimes we may feel like we're pushing all the right buttons but going nowhere (or even the wrong way).

How would our lives be different if we approached God with a "but if not" perspective on surrender? How much peace would we experience even when thrown into the fires of life? Two perspectives can help us adopt this ultimate posture:

First, it's not about the outcome but rather the journey itself. In John 14 when Thomas asks how the disciples will get to Jesus since they don't know where they are going. Jesus does not respond by telling them the GPS coordinates or any details about their final destination. He responds by saying, "I am the way." The path matters as much as the outcome. Are you focused on the way or pining for what's next?

Second, what matters most is that Jesus is with us in the fire. The fires of life will come. The furnace will burn extra hot sometimes. We can't avoid hardship, but we can bring Jesus into the flames. He's fireproof! And he can protect us from the heat.

We can't control the outcome, but if we apply these principles to the journey, we can be "unbound, walking in the midst of the fire, not hurt." Can you imagine journeying through the toughest parts of your life like this? We can't know how things will go, but we can decide how we will posture ourselves and who will go with us. If you want to live an exceptional life, aim to accept each twist and turn along the way with surrender and grace.

Pray about your encounter journey so far and ask for acceptance and presence right here where you're at.

I will not offer burnt offerings to the Lord that cost me nothing.
2 Samuel 24:24

Storyline: 2 Samuel 24

To put it mildly, David has a negative encounter with God. His decision to count the fighting men of Israel seems to be motivated by hubris. The only number that counted for defending Israel was the number one. One God who had protected David and his people without fail. The consequence of David's sin was a plague that stretched from north to south across Israel, killing 70,000 people in just a few days. The angel of the Lord who was tasked with carrying out this punishment is halted by God on a hilltop adjacent to the old city of Jerusalem. This hill was owned by a man named Araunah, who used it as a threshing floor. Chaff was often separated from wheat on hilltops where wind was abundant by throwing the cracked wheat into the air so the chaff could blow away.

Relieved and grateful, David ascends the hill to build an altar to ensure that the plague will be averted. But there's a problem. He does not own the hilltop. As king, he could have forcefully taken the land. Or perhaps, he could have made a temporary altar. He decides to buy the hilltop from Aruanah for a fair price. He refuses to make offerings that cost him nothing.

We love things that are cheap or free. We look for deals. We use discount codes. We take shortcuts whenever we can. There's nothing wrong with getting a deal on a pizza. But our desire for discounts can overflow into our relationship with God.

Are we looking to optimize our spirituality? Do we want to get the most out of the Bible while putting in the least? Are we short cutting our prayers? We are more resource and time wealthy than we probably even realize. Maybe even more than King David. We can life-hack some God time, or we can decide to use our time, resources, and attention to build something special with God. But we can't have it both ways.

If you've applied yourself to these devotionals over the last 30 days, you should be commended for your commitment to building with God. This has not been a small commitment. As you begin to move on to what's next in your walk with God, consider what a continued effort will do. David knew this: worship that costs nothing is worth nothing. Valuing and cultivating the presence of God in our lives is priceless.

Lifeline: Reaping the Results of Relationship

How will you cultivate the presence of God going forward? How will your efforts to draw near to God produce a harvest?

On the Mountain of the Lord
This isn't the first time we've visited Aruanah's hill during these devotionals. In fact, we've been on this mountain before and after David's encounter with the angel of the Lord. "Then Solomon began to build the house of the Lord in Jerusalem on Mount Moriah, where the Lord had appeared to David, his father, at the threshing floor of Ornan the Jebusite." (2 Chronicles 3:1)

This is the same mountain on which Abraham built his altar for Isaac, his son. He named it Moriah, "the Lord will see it through," when his sacrifice was halted, and a ram was substituted.

This is the same mountain that we traveled up to, singing the Songs of Ascents, that would later be called Mount Zion, the home of the temple and its sacrificial system. Solomon built the temple on the hilltop that David bought.

This place has a clear lesson for us: A real relationship with God requires sacrifice. Isaac, the price David paid, the temple. Maybe this was easier for our spiritual ancestors to conceptualize. There is no relationship without sacrifice. At the same time, shouldn't we understand this better than them? Isn't this the message of the cross? Without sacrifice, we cannot be in relationship with God.

What's your relationship with God worth to you? Take a moment to talk this out with God in prayer.

Tangibly, how much time, energy, and focus will you commit to building your relationship with God going forward? **Write down what you are willing to give to this relationship. What can God expect from you?**

In a sense, the story of the Bible is God putting on paper what he's willing to do to build a relationship with us. David's silver was a nice gesture, but it only secured a windblown piece of dirt and rock that's been fought over for centuries. The sacrifice of Isaac was significant, but a single ram was able to take his place. Even if we were to add up every sacrifice that ever occurred at the temple that Solomon built, we'd still have insufficient payment for our sin. It was on another hill, not too far away, Golgotha, the place of the skull, that God built his own altar of wood for sacrifice. Again, the message is clear: A real relationship with God requires sacrifice. And look what he was willing to give!

But they who wait for the Lord shall renew their strength.
Isaiah 40:31

Storyline: Isaiah 6:1-9, Isaiah 40

Isaiah's encounter with God happens while he's in "church". He's serving as a priest in the temple, and he is struck by a vision of God sitting on his throne with the train of his robe filling up the entire temple. There are seraphim singing as the voice of the Lord quakes and shakes the foundations of the temple. Isaiah is frozen in fear like a dead man. An angel touches his lips with a coal so his sins can be atoned for, allowing him to speak with God. God has a special mission for Isaiah, and Isaiah is ready, "Here am I! Send me."

Maybe this encounter experience has shaken your foundations in some way, big or small. We know about Isaiah's encounter with God because he wrote down his experience and listened to God in the days and years that followed. The prophetic songs he wrote after his encounter did more to inform God's people about the coming of the Messiah than any other writing in the Old Testament. Chapters 40-66 are a special section of prophecy that has come to be known as the Servant Songs because they so frequently reference God's servant (Messiah) who was to come.

Because Isaiah stayed attentive to the voice and presence of God after his encounter, the impact of his special meeting with God stretched beyond even his lifetime. Later generations who waited eagerly for God's redemption could know what to expect because of his writing. (Although, they often misunderstood the prophecies just as God told Isaiah they would.) John the Baptist gets his mission statement from Isaiah. (Isaiah 40:3) Jesus explains that he came to be a gentle ruler who would not hurt those who were already downtrodden. (42:2) The tragedy and victory of the cross is vividly detailed centuries before Jesus would walk the earth. (52:13-53:12) The prophecy of the passion in chapters 52-53 was written with so much detail that many doubters believed it must have been written after Jesus' death.

But in this, Isaiah's post-encounter experience has stretched all the way to our time. In the 1950's, a scroll of Isaiah was found at Qumran among the Dead Sea Scrolls. It has been dated to a century before Jesus' death on the cross. Today that scroll is displayed in the Israel Museum in Jerusalem, where it silently sings to all who visit that, "they who wait for the Lord shall renew their strength."

Lifeline: Post-Encounter

We see in the life and writings of Isaiah that God can stretch the impact of a special encounter across centuries. What will God do with your post-encounter experience?

It (isn't) Finished
You've made it to the last day of the Encounter devotionals, but you are far from done. This experience can be both life-changing and just the beginning. Take a moment to reflect and dream with God:

What is your biggest takeaway from these devotionals or the encounter experience?

How will you continue to grow in your relationship with God moving forward?

Who can you share this experience with? Write down and pray over a few names.

Dream about the future. How could this encounter change the world even after you're gone?

Look over the answers you just wrote down & craft them into a prayer to God.

An Invitation

While this devotional experience is certainly able to stand on its own as an invaluable resource for anyone desiring deeper communion with God, it is also intended to be used to ready individuals for a three-year immersive church curriculum driven by a podcast called Thread: Finding Your Place in God's Story. We invite you to listen on your favorite podcast platform or on YouTube. If you are a church leader or member who is interested in threading deep biblical teaching and life-changing spirituality into your congregation, check out the multitude of resources available at ThreadPodcast.org.

Made in the USA
Coppell, TX
10 January 2024

27538411R00056